THE AWAKENED HEART

THE
AWAKENED HEART

Opening Yourself to the Love You Need

GERALD G. MAY, M.D.

HarperSanFrancisco
A Division of HarperCollinsPublishers

FIRST HARPERCOLLINS PAPERBACK EDITION PUBLISHED IN 1993

Library of Congress Cataloging-in-Publication Data
May, Gerald G.
    The awakened heart : opening yourself to the love you need / Gerald G.
May. —1st HarperCollins pbk. ed.
        p.   cm.
    Includes bibliographical references and index.
    ISBN 0–06–065473–2 (pbk. : alk. paper)
    1. Christian life—1960–   2. Love—Religious aspects—Christianity.
3. Compulsive behavior—Religious aspects—Christianity. I. Title.
BV4501.2M418   1993   92–27083
248.4—dc20

04 05 RRD H 20 19 18 17 16 15

For Patricia Gibler Clark

"God, be my breath, my steps, my first word."
In your prayer and in your courage
you took the point for us
with boundless grace.

I sleep, but my heart is awake.

SONG OF SONGS 5:2

CONTENTS

Preface

*In the interior life we must never take our experiences as
the norm for everyone else.*
THE CLOUD OF UNKNOWING

There is much of my own experience in the text that follows.
My heart is in it as well, so at times I will speak as if my way
were the right way. If you find yourself disagreeing or unable to
identify with something I say here, do not miss a heartbeat
because of self-doubt. Seek your own experience; try to trust in
your authenticity and in what love seems to be calling forth
from your heart. Woven into the text are many questions to
help you clarify your experience; please spend a little time with
them.

Resources

If you wish some additional reading, I have listed plenty of
potentially helpful sources in the notes. Three small, unpreten-
tious works have been especially helpful for me. The first is
Brother Lawrence's *The Practice of the Presence of God*. A sixteenth-century Carmelite friar, Brother Lawrence pops up frequently in my writing and is responsible for identifying the four
ways of practice I describe in chapters 7–10. The second is
Thomas Kelly's *A Testament of Devotion*. Kelly was a twentieth-
century Quaker teacher with a special gift for describing radical
contemplative presence. The third is Thich Nhat Hanh's *Present*

Moment Wonderful Moment. Hanh, a Vietnamese Zen master who
was nominated for the Nobel Peace Prize by Dr. Martin Luther
King, Jr., is the author of several other beautiful little works as
well.

Scripture passages are cited in notes, but my quotations are
composites of several different translations. I recommend your
reading several translations of The Song of Songs, to which I
refer often and from which I have taken my title. The translations vary widely; I especially recommend Marcia Falk's beautiful new rendition. The facts of publication for this and the above
books are given in the notes.

I also make a number of references to the Shalem Institute. It
is an ecumenical organization supporting contemplative spirituality. If you would like information about its programs and
resources, write Shalem Institute for Spiritual Formation, Mount
Saint Alban, Washington, DC 20016. The Hebrew word *shalem*
is a cognate of *shalom* referring to wholeness. It is found in phrases
like *leb shalem,* a whole heart.[1]

Gratitude

I want to express gratitude to all the people of Shalem, who
enabled, supported, and empowered my writing in countless
ways, and especially to Tilden Edwards for his unfailing love. I
thank the following people who contributed vital comments on
early versions of the manuscript: Patricia Gibler Clark, Eileen
Tinsley Colbert, Carolyn Tanner Irish, Norma Jarrett Locher,
Marilyn Merikangas, and Leland Wilson. And as always I am
deeply grateful to my family, which keeps becoming more
extended: Betty, Earl, Denise, Paul, Kathie, Greg, Julie, and two
Sams. Thank you for your love, for your support, and for patient-
ly putting up with a "Mystickle Theologikan" in your lives.

More than any of my previous books, this one was surrounded by the heartfelt prayer of my spiritual friends. Those friends mean more to me than I can ever say. This book was as much theirs as mine. Now it is yours.

1

BEARING THE BEAMS OF LOVE

And we are put on earth a little space
That we might learn to bear the beams of love.
WILLIAM BLAKE

There is a desire within each of us, in the deep center of ourselves that we call our heart. We were born with it, it is never
completely satisfied, and it never dies. We are often unaware of
it, but it is always awake. It is the human desire for love. Every
person on this earth yearns to love, to be loved, to know love.
Our true identity, our reason for being, is to be found in this
desire.

I think William Blake was right about the purpose of humanity; we are here to learn to bear the beams of love. There are
three meanings of bearing love: to endure it, to carry it, and to
bring it forth. In the first, we are meant to grow in our capacity
to endure love's beauty and pain. In the second, we are meant to
carry love and spread it around, as children carry laughter and
measles. And in the third we are meant to bring new love into
the world, to be birthers of love. This is the threefold nature of
our longing.

You can find evidence of the longing in great art, music, liter-
ature, and religions; a common universal passion for love runs
through them all. Psychology offers evidence as well; the passion
for love can be found at the core of human motivation. There is

even evidence in neurology. The researcher Paul MacLean says the highly developed human cerebral cortex "makes possible the insight required to plan for the needs of others" and gives us "a concern for all living things."[1]

But for real proof you must look at your own longings and aspirations; you must listen to the deep themes of your own life story. In most of us the desire for love has often been distorted or buried, but if you look at your own life with honest and gentle eyes, you can discern it in yourself as a deep seeking of connectedness, healing, creation, and joy. This is your true identity; it is who you really are and what you exist for. You have your own unique experience of desiring love, but there is something universal about it as well; it connects you with all other human beings and with all of creation.

You probably already know your longing very well. You have felt it as hope for relationship, meaning, fulfillment, perhaps even a sense of destiny. Think for a moment about what has prompted you to do what you have done in life. When you have tried to be successful in your studies or work, what have you been seeking? When you have wanted to be pleasing, attractive, or helpful to others, what have you really been hoping for? Remember some moments in your life when you felt most complete and fulfilled; what did you taste there? Recall also feeling very bad, alone, worthless; what were you missing?

If you pause and look quietly inside, you may be able to sense something of your desire for love right now in this moment. Sometimes it is wonderful to touch this deep longing; it can seem expansive and joyful. At other times it can be painful, lonely, and even a little frightening. Whether it feels good or bad, its power and depth are awesome. When the desire is too much to bear, we often bury it beneath frenzied thoughts and activities or escape it by dulling our immediate consciousness of living. It is possible to run away from the desire for years, even decades, at a time, but we cannot eradicate it entirely. It keeps touching us in little glimpses and hints in our dreams, our hopes, our unguarded moments. We may go to sleep, but our desire for love does not. It is who we are.

Sometimes, in moments of quiet wonder, it is possible just to be with our desire. We can sense its power and beauty even when it aches for fulfillment. In truth it is an utterly simple thing. I can remember experiencing it in childhood, standing in a field and looking at the sky and just *being* in love. It wasn't love for any particular thing or person. It was more like being immersed in an atmosphere of love, feeling very alive, very present in the moment, intimately connected with everything around me.

Now and then we experience the same simplicity as adults. But for most of us it does not last very long. We have difficulty just being; we think we must get on with more important things. We have to be efficient. In becoming adults, we have been conditioned to believe that efficiency is more important than love.

Efficiency and Love

Efficiency is the "how" of life: how we meet and handle the demands of daily living, how we survive, grow, and create, how we deal with stress, how effective we are in our functional roles and activities.

In contrast, love is the "why" of life: why we are functioning at all, what we want to be efficient *for*. I cannot specifically define love, but I am convinced it is the fundamental energy of the human spirit, the fuel on which we run, the wellspring of our vitality. And grace, which is the flowing, creative activity of love itself, is what makes all goodness possible.

Love should come first; it should be the beginning of and the reason for everything. Efficiency should be "how" love expresses its "why." But it gets mixed up so easily. When I was a young parent, I wanted to take good care *of* my children (efficiency) because I cared so much *for* them (love). This was the way it should be. But soon I became preoccupied with efficiency. What were my kids eating? Were they getting enough sleep? Would we be on time for the car pool? My concerns about efficiency began to eclipse the love they were meant to serve. Getting to the car pool on time became more important than attending to a small fear or a hurt feeling. Too often the report card—the pre-eminent symbol of childhood efficiency—was more significant than the hopes and fears of the little one who brought it home.

It happens to all of us. Some people are so caught up in striving for efficiency that love seems like a luxury or even an obstacle to efficient functioning. Taken far enough, this makes for the ominous prospect of people who are very unloving and very efficient at what they do. For nearly a decade, Adolf Hitler was extremely efficient at expanding the Third Reich. A medical school professor I remember told his students that he found it more worthwhile to love his surgical successes than to love his patients. "As soon as you start feeling your patients' pain," he said, "you start losing your skill." He was only trying to help.

Just as people can be efficient without being loving, we all know people who are loving but not very efficient. Think for a moment about the most loving people you have known. By our modern criteria of success, how efficient were they? The people who have taught me the most about love have had more than their share of what we call dysfunction: self-doubt, suffering, and failure. I think of Brother Lawrence, the seventeenth-century monk who has inspired much of my writing. His biographers describe him as a bumbling, clumsy man who had difficulty even taking care of dishes in his monastery's kitchen. His brothers laughed at him. From the perspective of popular psychology, Brother Lawrence was inefficient and dysfunctional. He never quite achieved excellence in personal management. Yet what he gave to the cause of love is too great to be measured. After meeting him, the French theologian Fénelon described him as "gross by nature and delicate by grace." To be delicate by grace: to me that is more valuable than all the efficiency in the world.[2]

I also think of some of the people I cared for in psychiatric institutions. One day I ran out of matches for my pipe while interviewing a woman suffering from severe schizophrenia. She had not spoken before, but she broke through her hallucinations to ask the nurse for a light for me. In a prison ward, I was struggling to communicate with an aggressive, demanding patient. In a moment of frustration I glanced across the ward and noticed another man watching me. His eyes were so tender and understanding that I felt supported and encouraged without either of us saying a word. That man, suffering from paranoid delusions, had killed seven people. And he was caring for me. Both these people were dysfunctional in the extreme, yet grace flowed through them. We all know people of marginal efficiency who have touched our hearts with love. We might forget their names, or even where we met them, but their impact upon us remains forever.

Function and Dysfunction

If I could, I would take charge of my life and make it turn out just right. I can't. I have tried and failed repeatedly. I cannot adequately judge how loving I am, but I do know I lack efficiency. After considerable reflection, I have decided that I am dysfunctional in many ways.

Fully functional people are organized, disciplined, and able to get what they want out of life. Organization is out of the question for me; there are too many things going on, and they change so quickly I cannot keep up. The very idea of discipline makes me feel guilty. I have broken virtually every resolution I ever made. And as for getting what I want out of life, what I want most is love, and love comes only as a gift. All I can "do" is be willingly, actively open to receiving the gift.

I know love is a gift because I have experienced more love in my life than I could ever have deserved or earned. I cannot take credit for any of it. It is all grace. I have no doubt that a loving presence has abided with me over the years, mysteriously weaving love's presence through my aspirations and failures. I am too grateful for words.

Still, I cannot shake the feeling that I should have done it all by myself. Some tight, addicted voice inside me keeps saying, "You should be on top of things, in control; it is a cop-out to depend on grace." The voice is old and empty; I know it is not from my living heart. But it is powerful. For every failure in my life, I feel either guilt or shame, and sometimes both. Guilt says, "If only you had done it better." Shame says, "If only you had *been* better." After too many years of this, I admitted it. I am so dysfunctional I can't even figure out how to become functional. And it is all right.

It is better than all right, for it has been more my failures than my successes that have opened me to love. When I find myself being overconcerned with efficiency, I turn my attention to the mysterious, amazing grace that has seen me through all my dysfunctions. Sometimes I turn there because I need help. Sometimes

I turn in gratitude. But mostly, my turning toward grace is a simple, wordless act of love. Grace is love happening, love in action, and I have seen so much grace in the midst of so much brokenness in myself and others that I know we are all in love. We are in love, within love, as fish are in the sea and clouds are in the sky. It surrounds us, penetrates and perfuses us. In a very real sense, we are made of love. Love creates us, and we create love. I have felt it that way. I suspect you have felt it also, though it may have seemed too good to believe. For me, the fact that we are in love is far more important than the best of functioning. So most of the time when I try to attend to grace, I do it as an act of love. It is my response to being in love.

That is my experience. Yours is probably somewhat different. You have your own personality, your own addictions and aspirations, your own conditioning. In other words, you have your own ways of being dysfunctional. Similarly, you have your own ways of experiencing love and appreciating grace. Nevertheless, I am willing to bet that when you have your wits about you, you know that love is far more important than efficiency.

I doubt that anyone is perfectly functional. I have always known a few people who, at least on the surface, appear to have taken charge of their lives. They seem to know what they can control and what they cannot. They do not indulge in self-doubt. They do not procrastinate. They appear to have perfect marriages and problem-free children. They are helpful people, always ready to give me advice about how to get my own life in order. They would be wonderful company if they didn't make me feel like such a failure. But the real trouble is, I don't believe them.

Or is it that I don't believe myself? The perfectly functioning people are always people I do not know very well. When I get to know them, I see they are not so perfect. Then I look around for someone *else* who seems perfect. Why do I do this to myself? Maybe in some twisted, ironic way, feeling inferior to someone perfect gives me a hope for control. If they can do it, maybe I can too? I have tried to give this up, but occasionally I still look across the room at some financially solvent, upwardly mobile, blissful couple with perfect children and I wonder. I wonder about their efficiency and mine. I wonder about their love and mine.

Where Your Treasure Is

In most cases, thank God, love and efficiency are not mutually exclusive. It is entirely possible to use your money charitably and still balance your checkbook, though I have not yet achieved either. It should be possible for your work to contribute to the welfare of others and for you to receive adequate recompense for it, though most homemakers have yet to achieve it. We should be able to educate our children well while we are loving them, though in practice it sometimes feels impossible.

The problem is not whether we want love *or* efficiency; it is which we want *more*. Which do we give the higher priority? On the surface it seems natural to value love more highly. Nearly all the great institutions of our culture—religion, philosophy, art, even politics—give lip service, at least, to love as the supreme virtue. Most say that efficiency should exist only to serve the cause of love. The common sense of our human hearts says the same thing.

It is easy to say, but very difficult to put into practice. Individually and corporately, no matter how noble our words about love may sound, we are conditioned to believe efficiency is everything. Efficiency is the standard by which every person and enterprise is judged in our modern, developed culture. We weigh people's worth by how well they function. The value of blue collar workers is determined by their productivity. The worth of executives and professionals is based on their success. The merit of entertainers depends upon their draw at the box office. With such standards, the person disappears behind the product. We have even come to refer to children as "products" of their home environments.

We measure ourselves not by beginnings but by ends, not by what is in our hearts but by what we are able to accomplish. Even in marriages and families where we might most easily say, "I love you for who you are, not for how you look or what you do," we seldom act according to our words. Too often we disparage the spouse who fails to meet our expectations for attractiveness, entertainment, and affirmation of ourselves. Too often we scorn the child who does something wrong and says, "I didn't mean to."

But there is a worse thing. Our society encourages us to believe that love is just another function, an ability to be learned and refined. There are techniques for love, we are told, and if we love efficiently we will have something to show for it: well-managed, smoothly functioning relationships, social popularity, emotional security, sexual fulfillment. Seen in this light, expressions of love become commodities, loved ones become objects, and the pains of love become problems to be solved. In therapy, people have told me, "I don't know how to love," or, "I think I am incapable of loving." What sadness! No one is incapable of loving. We all have difficulty expressing love; it would not be love if it didn't cause us trouble. To some extent we are all afraid of love; we do not want to be hurt. Sometimes people become so afraid or embittered that they are indeed paralyzed in expressing or perceiving love. But everyone loves. No matter how much trouble we have expressing or appreciating it, love is inescapable; it is what causes us to care. "Was it not love," I asked my patients, "that wounded you in the first place? And is it not your love that makes you care enough to miss it now?"

Let me say it again; no one is incapable of loving. When it comes to love, *capability* is the wrong word entirely. Capability is competence at performing a function. There is much I do not know about love, but of this I am certain: love is not a function. It is a quality of being that exists beneath and before all our functions. The word we must use is *capacity.* Capacity implies space; it refers to how much we can hold, perhaps how much we can bear. This has much to do with love. Machines have capabilities; vessels have capacity. Love is always with us, seeking to fill us to our capacity.

If we give love primacy, if we claim it as our true treasure, there will still be plenty of room to develop our capabilities, our efficiency. But with efficiency as the ruling standard there is little or no space for love; we are led to doubt the value of love and our capacity for it.

When we hold efficiency as our primary value, we expect to achieve control, success, and security on our own terms. Even when our expectations are not met, we still believe we will come out secure and satisfied if we just do things differently, learn more, or make ourselves better in some way. Thus we make a god of efficiency, an idol of success, a deity of achievement. These are the false gods that tell us we should be gods ourselves: in charge of our lives.

By worshiping efficiency, the human race has achieved the highest level of efficiency in history, but how much have we grown in love? Are we really any more graceful than our forebears were? The nations of our world have taken some significant steps toward freedom and justice, but at the same time technology has made us more destructive to one another and our planet. I do not know how the balance works out, whether we are really becoming more loving. But it is clear that our love has not kept up with our efficiency; we have too often sacrificed love for progress.

The Invitation of Love

If we want to set the relationship between efficiency and love in its rightful order, we must go beyond laws and proclamations. If we desire a more loving society, we individual persons must return to the deepest common sense of our hearts; we must claim love as our true treasure. Then comes the difficult part: we must try to live according to our desire in the moment-by-moment experiences of our lives.

There is nothing more beautiful and freeing than living with conscious dedication to love. The way of love invites us to become vessels of love, sharers in grace rather than controllers of achievement. It invites us toward increasing freedom from all our slaveries and addictions. It encourages us to ease our grasping and striving for false security. It asks for vulnerability rather than self-protection, willingness instead of mastery. It beckons us toward participation in the great unfolding of creation, toward becoming one with it rather than standing apart and trying to overcome it.

But the invitation of love is as challenging as it is beautiful. Whether you have in mind such wide goals as reshaping human rights and world values, or something as intimate as simple gratitude for the grace in your own life, saying yes to the invitation of love will hurt you. Living for love requires openness to love itself, a radical vulnerability to consciously being in love. To claim this is to enter a gentle warfare against immense internal and external forces. The enemy is that which would stifle your love: your fear of being hurt, the addictions that restrict your passion, and the efficiency worship of the world that makes you doubt the value of love. It is warfare because these forces are very real and very threatened by love. They will fight to keep their power. But the warfare must be gentle on your part; your only weapon is love itself. It feels more vulnerable than David facing Goliath. David had a sling and knew how to use it, but love can never be used. It can only be embraced and trusted. Love does not conquer all, because *conquer* is the wrong word entirely.

I am not exaggerating. Choosing love will open spaces of immense beauty and joy for you, but you will be hurt. You already know this. You have retreated from love countless times in your life because of it. We all have. We have been and will be hurt by the loss of loved ones, by what they have done to us and we to them. Even in the bliss of love there is a certain exquisite pain: the pain of too much beauty, of overwhelming magnificence. Further, no matter how perfect a love may be, it is never really satisfied. The very fulfillment of a desire sparks our passion for more; sooner or later we discover a deepened yearning within what felt like satisfaction. Even in their beauty, the beams of love can often seem too much to bear.

In both joy and pain, love is boundless. Love is open, allowing our hearts to be touched and moved by what exists. Love is honest, willing to be present to life just as it is, in all its beauty and ugliness. True love is not blind at all; it sees what is and feels it as it is with no rose-colored glasses and no anesthesia.

No Justification, No Defense

We know in our hearts that choosing love is choosing life and freedom; saying yes to love's invitation is the only way to lasting meaning and real worth. But our minds are likely to have a different opinion. The parts of our minds that are addicted to efficiency will make us doubt our desire. They will demand to know why we want to risk being hurt in the cause of love. What purpose will it serve? What function? Would it not be better to seek safety and security and simply hope for a little joy now and then, a few touches of caring along the way?

Our minds may point out, very accurately, that we will never be "successful" at love. We will never make ourselves all-loving, nor will we vanquish the forces of efficiency worship in this world. We cannot expect even to conquer our own petty addictions; we have tried before and failed. If our minds are wise, they will also warn us not to expect satisfaction of our desire for love. Love is relentless, even ruthless; every taste of love we experience leaves us yearning for more.

These are hard questions and criticisms, made even more difficult because they are valid. And there is very little we can say in response to them. Whether the challenge comes from our own minds or from other people around us, we cannot justify or defend our yes to love. What kind of explanation can we give? All we can honestly say is, "I just want to." Inside, we may know it is the great passion of our life and that it is somehow meant for everyone. But from the outside it may sound like nothing more than a whim, a childish idealism, perhaps even selfishness.

Beyond Psychology

There really is no justification we can give, no defense against the challenge. Today many people try to give psychospiritual justifications: "Meditation helps me concentrate on my work." "Faith in Christ gives me peace of mind." "My belief in a Higher Power is enabling my recovery from addiction." "In searching for my true self, I am becoming more whole and healthy." Such statements may be true, but they miss the point of love. Love cannot be a means to any end. Love does not promise success, power, achievement, health, recovery, satisfaction, peace of mind, fulfillment, or any other prizes. Love is an end in itself, a beginning in itself. Love exists only for love.

The invitation of love is not a proposal for self-improvement or any other kind of achievement. Love is beyond success and failure, doing well or doing poorly. There is not even a right and wrong way. Love is a gift. One can never be proud of being in love. One can only be grateful.

Beyond Morality

Neither is the invitation of love a moral commandment to be followed because of fear or obligation. Every religion has moral commandments intended to promote kindness toward others. Ideally, following such principles is both a practice for love and an expression of love, but it is only a small part of love's invitation. For example, I may act lovingly toward my neighbor because I am afraid of feeling guilty or of going to hell. The actions may be good, but they come from fear, not love. The real commandment of love is an invitation born in our own yearning, not an externally imposed "should."

Jews and Christians honor the great commandments to love God with one's entire being, and one's neighbor as oneself. The very name of Islam implies surrendering completely to God. The heart of the Hindu Song of God, the *Bhagavad-Gita,* is God's request for complete, unconditional love. Buddhists seek the inherent compassion existing at the root of reality. There is much more here than law and precept. In all these deep traditions of faith, love calls for a dedication of one's whole life, a consecrated self-giving so complete that the human will can never accomplish it. Because it is beyond the will, it is beyond all moral codes of behavior. In every deep world religion, the greatest commandment goes to the very core of being, and there it depends radically upon grace.

At this level, the commandment of love is no regulation; it is a statement of the truth of life. It is an invitation to accept love's passion, commit oneself to it, and try to live it wholeheartedly. The greatest commandments are not obligations at all, but affirmations of grace. They are promises that with our willing assent, grace will make possible the triumph of full, unfettered love within us.

Our assent, our yes, finally comes from nothing other than our own yearning, from passion itself. It may surface temporarily as desire for self-improvement, functional efficiency, moral virtue, or social justice, but ultimately it will take us beyond and beneath all such ends. Love will bring us to our ever-present beginning, where our only reason for saying yes is simply that we want to. Here it is only our plain desire that makes true assent possible: the desire to respond to a larger love already given, the desire to love and to be loved and to be fully, consciously present in love as an end in itself. It is a matter of simple caring, our hearts aching for the fullness of love for no other reason than its own essential goodness. In this simple, exquisite longing, awakening in each precious moment, we know who we really are. It is the likeness of God.

Identity

We in modern Western culture have gone just a little bit crazy about finding out who we really are. From psychological individuation to genealogical roots, from archetypes and mythology to masculine and feminine identity, from personality typing to astrology, from addiction recovery to childhood abuse recovery, we go from fad to fad asking, "Who am I, and who am I meant to become?"

There is something fundamentally good about this cultural identity crisis. We are no longer satisfied with being identified solely by what we do: "I am a real estate salesman"; or by our relationships: "I am Frank's wife"; or by our attributes: "I am an African-American Protestant Gemini who loves conversation and good music." We know there is more to us than that. We know our true dignity does not depend upon our descriptions of ourselves.

It is healthy and humane to seek a deeper sense of who we are. But the search has become frantic, a maze of blind passages. As I write this, the addiction recovery movement has itself become a major addiction for thousands of people. People struggle to find dysfunction in their families or abuse in their childhoods so they can join the recovering throngs. Some, perhaps many, are struggling with "memories" of childhood abuse that never even happened. Whenever things become so desperate and complicated, we have usually overlooked something simple. In this case we have overlooked the immediate experience of our desire. By excessive concern for where we have come from and where we can or should go, we miss the simple truth of our here and now.

In all my studies of psychology and spirituality, I have found hope for real wholeness only in the human heart's desire for love in the present moment. The experience is utterly simple. It exists before any words or symbols are applied to it, and it *is* who we are. In one silent breath, the love-force in us gives us our identity and draws us toward our home and destiny. We are created by love, to live in love, for the sake of love. Out of this simple ground arise all our beautiful differences; love expresses itself in delicious diversity in our different families and cultures, in women and in men, in the young and the old, and in each human being's unique personality and history. We are endlessly diverse and unique in our hues and textures, but we are also all one; love is expressing itself not only through us but *as* us.

One's essential identity is not to be found in one's ancestors or archetypes, one's gender or race, one's childhood experiences or adult accomplishments. Such attributes are only expressions of a simpler, deeper truth. They are the tones, instruments, cadences, and chords of the human symphony, arising fresh in each moment, sounding through time. The sound may seem harmonious or discordant, sweet or harsh, but it is one song of love.

It is not easy to own and claim love as our true identity and deepest dignity. We cannot describe it in words. We cannot grasp it or treat it as an object. It is not something we can do, a process to go through, or even a specific way to be. It transcends psychological categorization, philosophical comprehension, and even moral judgment. The only way to own and claim love as our identity is to fall in love with love itself, to feel affection for our longing, to value our yearning, treasure our wanting, embrace our incompleteness, be overwhelmed by the beauty of our need.

In other words, the invitation of love is to be consciously, energetically alive and involved *in* love. This is the real meaning of in*vita*tion: living in, living into, being alive within. Infinite possibilities of action spring forth from such immediate aliveness in love, action that is right for the situations in which we find ourselves, action that is peacemaking, justice-bringing, and healing for our world.

What is the nature of the action that is called forth from being in love? I have said it is not a means toward an end, not self-improvement, not moral obligation. I think we have to say it is a response. Love invites response, *needs* response. The actions that arise from loving presence are responses of love to love in the situation at hand. There is something absolutely natural about it, and it is no passive, sedentary thing. It is not simply a cycle of feelings. Love responding to love is the ground of all creation. Here longing brings forth union, and union births creation. New things are formed, separating from the old, aching for reunion. Things change, grow, collapse, heal, die, and are reborn in freshness. This is the doing of being, the how of the why, all happening within "a holy energy that fills the universe, playing like lightning."[3]

Desire is the essential human experience in this great cosmic play of love. Beyond all ways and means, desire is our one human resource for love. It is our passion, our life force, our spirit. We can neither create it nor make it go away. Our desire *is* our love. In affirming our desire we finally know who we are, and we know our place in things. We are needed, necessary, and beautiful.

It is out of this pristine ground of the heart that true assent and identity must finally come, stripped of external justification and rational explanation. The questions of efficiency have no meaning at this heart level. Efficiency asks, "Why do you say yes?" We can only answer, "Because I want to." Efficiency comes back with, "But for what reason, and to what end?" And we can only say, "The only reason is my desire, and to that there is no end."

2

THE LIFE OF THE HEART

> Love is the life of our heart. According to it, we desire,
> rejoice, hope and despair, fear, take heart, hate, avoid
> things, feel sad, grow angry, and exult.
> FRANCIS DE SALES

Love is the most important quality of human life, and the least comprehensible. I am a little embarrassed to think how much time and energy I have spent trying to understand love. Perhaps I believed my concepts and definitions of love would help me "do" it better or make it more safe. No such luck. I do not think we can ever adequately define or understand love; I do not think we were ever meant to. We are meant to participate in love without really comprehending it. We are meant to give ourselves, live ourselves into love's mystery.

It is the same for all important things in life; there is a mystery within them that our definitions and understandings cannot grasp. Definitions and understandings are images and concepts created by our brains to symbolize what is real. Our thoughts about something are never the thing itself. Further, when we think logically about something, our thoughts come sequentially—one after another. Reality is not confined to such linearity; it keeps happening all at once in each instant. The best our thoughts can do is try to keep a little running commentary in rapid, breathless sequence.

Because our thoughts, images, and concepts are only symbols and commentaries, we can get into trouble when we mistake them for reality. For example, if we try to conform ourselves to our self-concepts, we become neurotic, living according to our images. Similarly, if we cling to solid images of God, we wind up worshiping our thoughts about God instead of God. This is a spiritual neurosis, an idolatry of the mind. In the same way, we confuse and restrict ourselves when we try to love according to our ideas about love.

We may think, for example, that love is some combination of helpful action, tender feelings, committed relationship, and romance. These are indeed aspects of love, but they bear about as much resemblance to love itself as raindrops to weather or waves to the sea. To the extent that we try to love according to such forms, we suffer from both psychological and spiritual neurosis. Psychologically, we cannot be fully ourselves in love; spiritually, we miss love's holy mystery.

A certain asceticism of mind, a gentle intellectual restraint, is needed to appreciate the important things in life. To be open to the truth of love, we must relinquish our frozen comprehensions and begin instead to appreciate. To comprehend is to grasp; to appreciate is to value. Appreciation is gentle seeing, soft acknowledgment, reverent perception. Appreciation can be a pleasant valuing: being awed by a night sky, touched by a symphony, or moved by a caress without needing to understand why. It can also be painful: feeling someone's suffering, being shocked by loss or disaster without comprehending the reason. Appreciation itself is a kind of love; it is our direct human responsiveness, valuing what we cannot grasp. Love, the life of our heart, is not what we think. It is always ready to surprise us, to take us beyond our understandings into a reality that is both insecure and wonderful.

Your Love Story

Instead of trying to know what love is by abstract concepts and definitions, I suggest you seek a more direct appreciation of your own experiences of love. You might think of it as telling your story of love. Begin with a few broad brush strokes about what love has been for you in your life so far. Recall some experiences of love for people, places, possessions. What did those experiences of love feel like? How did they affect you? What is your experience of love right now? How do you sense yourself loving, being loved, being in love? And what are your desires for love: your hopes, dreams, and fantasies?

Love appears with endless variety: kindness, attraction, commitment, sexuality, intimacy, concern, simple appreciation, on and on. There are good feelings like tenderness, connectedness, and warmth. And there are unpleasant feelings like grief, loneliness, and fear. See if you can appreciate the range of feelings that accompany love for you, your sense of the depth and breadth of love. Then, very quietly, ask what all these feelings might have in common. What is it that makes you call it love? What is the basic quality of loving someone or something? What is it to be loved?

Now see if you can recall an experience of just being in love, when love became radically free for you. One person experienced it while watching a sunset: "I just sat there, absorbed by the beauty. It was not simply the sunset; it was everything and everyone. It felt as though I had fallen in love with everything." Another person related it to romance: "Sometimes when I was with him, things would just open up. I don't know how else to say it. I felt I was in love with the whole world, and it loved me." Still another talked about worship: "There are times when the routine of ritual falls away and I'm just there, and everyone is there, and the whole world is there, all one in love." Yet another spoke of childhood: "I can't quite remember, but I know the feeling. Maybe I'd be playing in the sun, or lying on my bed, and just feel so warm, as if I were being held." Some people cannot actually recall such experiences, but instead sense a kind of background knowledge, an awareness that something like this does exist somewhere, and always has. Whatever your experience, try to be honest with it and appreciate it as fully as you can.

Action, Knowing, and Feeling

If you find it difficult to identify with the examples I have given, it may be that you associate love more with action or knowledge than with feelings. Classic Eastern and Western spiritual traditions identify three ways of approaching life: the way of action, the way of knowing, and the way of feeling. It is assumed that a full life involves all three, but at any given time a person tends to prefer one. It is not important to do psychological gymnastics to figure out which orientation you might have. It is critical, however, to recognize that neither love nor anything else of consequence can rightfully be reduced to one narrow vision. Love is feeling—tenderness, caring, and longing—but it is also much more. Love is action—kindness, charity, and commitment—and again, it is much more. Love is knowing—openness of attitude, realization of connectedness, expansion of attention beyond ourselves—and still it is more.

Reflect once again on your experiences of love from the standpoints of action and knowing as well as feelings. What are some of the activities, the doings, of love for you? What are the knowings, the attitudes and realizations, the wisdom of love? Don't try to pull these insights into any final answer; just let them embellish your story.

Love is always more than our actions can do, more than our knowings can understand, and more than our feelings can bear. Doing loving acts, however helpful, is not enough. Thinking loving thoughts, however charitable, is not enough. Feeling loving feelings, however tender, is not enough. Put them all together, and love still wants more. Give us time, and we will want more love. Give love time, and it will want more of us.

Contemplation: The Fourth Way

In both Eastern and Western spirituality, there is a fourth way, an appreciation that embraces action, feeling, and knowing and also seeks the "more" that love always is. In Hinduism it is known as the Royal Way; in Tibetan Buddhism it is the Way of Total Completeness. In the West, it is called the contemplative way.[1]

Contrary to popular understanding, contemplation does not imply quietness or withdrawal. Instead, it is a quality of immediate, open presence that is directly involved with life-as-it-is. Recall some of the moments in your life when you have felt most alive, most awake, most completely present and involved with what was going on. Some may be the same times you identified as just being in love. Others may be surprises. People often experience flashes of contemplation in prayer and meditation, but it can happen anywhere. One person described "perfect presence" when there was a fire in her house and she acted immediately to take care of her family and call for help. "I never felt so alive" she said, "and until after it was all over, there was no fear—none at all." Another woman described the same thing during childbirth. A man told of contemplative presence that happened spontaneously while he was waiting in an airport for a delayed flight. "Normally I would have been restless, but for some reason, in some strange way, I was just *there*, with all the people in their joys of reunion and griefs of separation, with the real lives of the airline personnel, even with the trucks and trees outside the windows, and the person making announcements on the public address system. God, if only I could live all my days like that!"

Contemplative moments can happen in crisis, excitement, and great activity, or in quiet stillness and simple appreciation. However it happens, contemplation immerses us in the reality of the moment. We are no longer standing apart and reflecting upon our experience. We are vitally, consciously involved with what is going on. Everything is more clear, more real than it usually is.

I do not know how well I have described contemplation; your own remembrance is better than my words. Go over your experience again. What is the difference between the way you are most of the time and the way you have been in those special moments of immediate presence? Why is it that the moments seem to come so rarely? Where are you the rest of the time?

For now, let us say contemplation is a conscious willingness to fully enter into life just as it is. Manjusrimitra, an ancient saint of Tibetan Buddhism, called it "pure and total presence." Thomas Kelly, a twentieth-century American Quaker, called it "continually renewed immediacy." The contemplative way recognizes that love or any other aspect of life cannot be fully appreciated through acting, knowing, feeling, or any combination of the three. It admits that human experience can never stand apart and completely comprehend truth. It celebrates the always-present, ungraspable mystery in life.[2]

The contemplative way acknowledges that we begin to appreciate love's fullness only as we enter it immediately, directly, and with undefended awareness. This happens very simply, not by any thought or strategy, but by being present *in* love: being appreciatively and responsively right here and now. It happens as we realize our aliveness in the present moment. Rabbi Abraham Isaac Kook, a modern master of the spiritual life, described contemplation "not as a dim configuration that is presented to you from the distance, but as the reality in which you live." The twelfth-century Islamic saint Ibn al-'Arabi said that "when the Heart embraces the Reality, it is as if Reality fills the Heart."[3]

I am proposing that contemplative appreciation is the fullest possible realization of love. The contemplative moments that come to us all as flashes of immediate presence are glimpses of the way life yearns to be lived. They are hints of the vast, graceful gift of love that has already been given to the family of humanity. The contemplative heart says, "Only open your hands, receive the gift." This does not mean we can control contemplation or that we can be contemplative at will. It is a gift that we can accept only as it is given. But it is given far more frequently, far more steadily than we could ever imagine.

I will have much more to say about contemplation as we proceed, but with this sense of it as a background, I want to offer three visions of love, three dimensions of love's mystery. In the first, we will look at falling in love and being in love. In the second, we will explore how attachment and addiction blend with love's desire for freedom. In the third, we will consider a more cosmic vision: love in the context of stability and creation. Keep in mind that these discussions are not meant to explain love or to figure it out. They are meant to be touched lightly, only to appreciate the depth and breadth of love more fully.

Falling in Love and Being in Love

Love pervades our existence in an endless procession of actions, thoughts, and feelings. It is present in any desire, in all feelings of attraction, in all caring and connectedness. It embraces us in precious moments of immediate presence. It is also present whenever we experience loneliness, loss, grief, and rejection. We may say such feelings of bereavement come from the absence of love, but in fact they are signs of our loving; they express how much we care. We grieve according to how much of ourselves we have already given; we yearn according to how much we would give, if only we could.

We may try to learn techniques or use strategies to ease our yearning for love. We may assume love is somewhere other than right here, and we may search for it, following a variety of psychological or spiritual road maps. But when we do find love, we discover it by falling into it. And it is never quite what we expected.

We think of falling in love as a rare occurrence, but it is the most ordinary of human events. We do it all the time. We fall in love whenever we give ourselves to someone or something. We have fallen in love with everyone and everything we hold dear: with people, objects, activities, thoughts, feelings, hopes, memories, beliefs, even with attitudes and moods.

Each time we lose one of these dear things—or even think about losing it—we recognize how precious it is to us. We realize how we have fallen in love with it. Even if it were possible to go through life without loving another person—and I feel certain it is not—we could only achieve it by loving our aloneness. It is just not possible to live without loving.

Falling in love is as ordinary and normal as our breathing. But it is also always special. It is special because it wakes us up. It thrills us and hurts us and makes us conscious of being alive. It lets us know that no matter how dull or distracted our minds may have been, our hearts are wide awake.

We can categorize love in endless ways, devise countless strategies to make it happen as we wish, yet always it remains beyond our control. We know that love is beyond our control because it keeps hurting us. We would like to experience the joy and energy of love without being vulnerable to its pain, but there is no way to do that. To love is to care, to care is to give ourselves, and giving ourselves means being willing to be hurt.

More than the surprises of love, I think it is our vulnerability to love, the impossibility of controlling it or securing ourselves within it, that causes us to speak of "falling" in love. In love, we fall from our pride, from our sense of mastery and separateness, from whatever towers of false safety we have constructed for ourselves. We fall into wonder and wakefulness, joy and agony.

The vulnerability that love requires often makes us shy away. Especially if we have been recently or severely hurt by love, we are wary of falling again too soon. We erect defenses around our hearts and dull our awareness of being. Some wisdom inside us knows it is impossible to love safely; we either enter it undefended or not at all. For a while then, we choose against love. We feel that the bliss of love is not worth the pain that comes with it. Temporarily, we choose the safety of dullness; we suppress our desire.

It is possible to maintain such defenses for a long time. But sooner or later, in some unpredictable way, our hearts wake us up. The sparks of desire rekindle within us. We begin to live again. We are more open, more vulnerable to falling. We may still be very much afraid, but our defenses have begun to melt. We hear again the wisdom of our hearts saying, "Love does hurt, but it is worth it."

Falling in love is worth it because it is the doorway into *being* in love. It is the place where love invites us into itself. Once we have fallen, if we can trust enough, be vulnerable enough to wake up and see where we are, the distinctions blur between lover and beloved. Love no longer has such a clear me and you, no distinct origin and end. Precious moments of presence come more frequently, and it is called communion. Falling in love has two; being in love has one. Falling in love temporarily fills a space, a capacity, within us, but being in love opens that space into infinity.[4]

If we look for it, we can find the invitation to be in love wherever we have fallen. It exists in all our loves: not just in passion or compassion for other people, but also where we have given ourselves to objects, behaviors, doctrines, and anything else that stimulates our desire. It is present even in the loves we would rather deny: love of power, love of money, even love of violence. The invitation of love is limited by no social, psychological, or religious distinctions. It does not restrict itself to noble causes. It is present wherever we find ourselves caring deeply, whenever something really matters to us.

Once again think of your own experience. What are some of the vulnerabilities that love has created in you? When have the beauty and the pain of love seemed too much to bear? How have you tried to protect yourself against love, and what has that done to your sense of aliveness? How have you fallen again, and how has that affected your consciousness of living, your awareness of the moment? What, for you, is the relationship between falling in love and being in love?

Addiction and Freedom

Falling in love often feels choiceless; it seems to break through our defenses, sometimes even against our will. Being in love, however, is something we say yes to. It is a willing yielding into love's presence. It is a conscious easing of defenses. When we accept the presence of love and give ourselves to it, we glimpse immense freedom and spaciousness. There is room to move around, unencumbered by fear and doubt. Being in love is like a breath of liberation for our spirits. It awakens our passion and inspires a vitality within us that we never knew we had. Love always seeks freedom; love wants to play.

But the pure freedom of love seldom lasts. Something creeps in and mercilessly restrains it. The something is addiction. This is the second vision of love's mystery; addiction opposes the freedom of love. I have described the opposition at length in *Addiction and Grace,* but let me summarize it here. Addictions come from a process that is inherent in the functioning of the cells of our brains and bodies. Psychologically, the process is called *conditioning;* the spiritual term is *attachment.* Attachment nails the energy of our passion to someone or something, producing a state of addiction. Once addiction takes hold, the loved one becomes an object to which we are bound. The object of addiction may be anything: a person, a place, a substance, a behavior, a belief. We come to expect gratification from this object and to want more and more of it. Sooner or later we realize that we have not only fallen for this thing, we are in bondage to it. Whether we call it dependence or codependence, we have been given away as choicelessly as if sold by a master we never knew existed. Our love, which held such promise of unconditional freedom, has become conditioned and conditional.[5]

It is unpleasant to recognize that addiction can so invade and undermine the freedom of love. It is even more offensive to realize that no abiding human love is completely free from addiction. Addiction finds its way into all our loves. We can discern how much by asking ourselves two questions about freedom. They are hard questions, but I believe we must face them. Walk with me now, with a little gentle courage.

The first freedom question is this: How free are we to give up the persons or things we love? Relinquishment is painful in any love; the deeper the love, the more painful the letting go. We truly lose a part of ourselves when we lose a loved one. To the extent we are free, we know we could bear that pain. As we become more addicted, however, the relinquishment seems increasingly impossible. We feel we would lose not just a part of ourselves but our very selves. We feel we could not go on.

Our most addicted loving is our most desperate loving. We have all had occasion to feel something like "I cannot live without you," "If I don't get that promotion, my life is over," "Everything depends on buying that house," or "I can't think of anything but that mistake I made." It happens in loves that we call good, like love for spouse or children. It happens in loves we label bad, like substance abuse and workaholism. Good or bad, delicious or disgusting, our most addicted loves feel heavy and ponderous, obsessed and compelled, devoid of freedom. We can be obsessed by things as great as allegiance to family or country, or as small as keeping a new car undented. We can be compelled by things as noble as peace and justice or as petty as power and greed.

It is such addicted loving, I believe, that breeds human violence on our planet. In a psychiatric hospital I remember talking with the boyfriend of a young woman who had attempted suicide. "I guess she must really love me," he said, "because she tried to kill herself when I left her." The very next day another woman spoke of another boyfriend: "He really does love me; you should have seen how he tried to kill that guy who was coming on to me." Take the same kind of addiction, expand the number of people involved, and you have war. I believe every war can be traced to conflicting addictions to possessions, ideology, territory, or ways of life. Sometimes violence and war become addictions in themselves. In the film *Patton,* the general, so efficient because of his extraordinary compulsion, looks over the smoking wreckage of a battlefield and whispers, "God forgive me, I do love it so."

The second freedom question, just as painful, is this: How free are we *within* our love? How much space is there for us to be ourselves? To what extent can we play? How much is our freedom confined, restricted, perhaps even imprisoned, by our attachment to the person or thing we love?

Our most addicted loving is our most choiceless loving: "I cannot tell her how I feel because she would leave me," or worse, "I cannot tell him because he would beat me." It may be hard to admit, but we have all had experiences of giving away our power, sacrificing our dignity, compromising our principles, putting up with something we knew was destructive for the sake of addicted love. In one way or another, we all know what it is to relinquish our freedom for love.

It is critical to understand what freedom means here. Because love is a giving of ourselves, it always involves some choice to direct and restrain our behavior. Love means being willing to make sacrifices for someone or something. When we love, we do not follow every impulse that comes along. We have a higher concern, a deeper desire; we value our beloved more than we value our passing whims. The freedom question, then, is not whether we can do whatever we want but whether we can do what we *most deeply* want.

It is a critical distinction; please take care to understand it. The difference is between attachment binding desire and commitment honoring desire. It is the difference between codependence and compassion, between neediness and mutuality, between shame and dignity.

Only we ourselves are responsible when we sell out our freedom: when we put up with abuse, when we abuse ourselves with substances, when we do destructive things in order to maintain our jobs, relationships, possessions, or self-images. Yet it is not a simple matter of willpower or strength of character. We are responsible for our addictive behavior, but we feel powerless to control it. If anything is hell for the human will, this is. And if we are to recognize our dependence on grace anywhere, it is here. We see it whenever we hit rock bottom with our addictions, when they bring us to our knees and convince us we cannot master them. Then we realize only a larger love can save us, a love beyond our own wills, a love more powerful than any addiction.

In the atmosphere of addiction, the invitation to be in love becomes radically more important. It is no longer a spiritual luxury, a holiness reserved for saints and eccentrics. Now being in love becomes thoroughly practical and absolutely essential. It is our lifeline. It is our life.

Even in the depths of addiction—and perhaps more there than anywhere else—love's invitation toward freedom keeps coming to us. No matter how caught up in addiction we have been, we have all felt the freedom of choosing to respond to another's need for no good reason—for no reason other than that the need was there. We have experienced the wonder of giving ourselves to something beautiful, not because we had to, but just because it so attracted us. We may not believe it, but all of us have even tasted the sheer grace of being loved for no other reason than that we are who we are. In each of these moments, the lover is free to say yes or no, and chooses, quite wonderfully, to say yes. Sometimes, very simply, we have just loved being alive—the spaciousness is so vast, the freedom so immense, the love so unconditioned.

There is a spectrum of love's freedom. At one extreme, attachment binds the energy of love, making slaves of lovers and objects of loved ones. At the other extreme are tastes of unconditioned love, communion as an end in itself, a being in love that is given freely and grows freedom within us. All our loves reflect this spectrum, blending a certain bondage with moments of great liberty.

Watch two lovers at the beach. They walk closely and slowly, open to all the sights and sounds around them, enjoying the feeling of their togetherness. They play like children. There are many moments of just being in love. Then they separate a little, looking for shells, each trusting in the abiding presence of the other. Their freedom is great, but it is not boundless; there is a limit to how far they will go apart. At some point one will relinquish his or her own path and return to join the other. Like the ocean by their side, their romance ebbs and flows with freedom and attachment. Yet it is all one experience of love.

Our loves for work, possessions, habits, and substances weave the same tapestry of liberation and restriction. Overeating might release us for a moment from the oppression of inner emptiness, but in the next it imprisons us in self-hatred. Our quests for power and attractiveness may let us escape the feeling of being ignored, but only at the cost of endless striving. Mature married love frees us from relational striving and gives us security and moments of true communion, but passion and excitement wane, captivated by habit. Love is a delicious confusion; it reveals our most extreme limitations and our most holy aspirations, all in one impossibly agonizing and wonderful experience of living.

Stability and Creation

It is a temptation now to slip back into efficiency mind and try to find a way to keep all our loves unattached. There must be a way to achieve perfection: complete freedom from addiction, endless unconditionality. But the third vision of love's mystery is this: There is a rightness to our vision of perfection, but there is also a rightness to the struggle in which we currently find ourselves.

We cannot achieve freedom for love. Addiction is so embedded in our physical makeup that completely free human love is a disembodied fantasy. Like many other people, I have tried to envision what completely unattached love would look like. To be sure, the freedom would be magnificent. But I wonder what the freedom could be *for*, without an even greater freedom to seek, without growth toward something always better, without the pain of yearning and the joy of creation.

A story is told about Marpa, one of the great enlightened masters of Tibetan Buddhism. His son had been killed, and he was very upset. His disciples found him crying. "You have told us that everything is illusion," the disciples said. "How about the death of your son? Isn't that also an illusion?" "True," Marpa replied, "but my son's death is a super-illusion."[6]

Love does not find its fullness in achieving complete nonattachment nor in any other kind of perfection. Love's deepest realization is found in growing, struggling, moving, longing, reaching *toward* perfection while living life fully as it is in the here and now. I used to think of heaven as a place of perfect repose, endless serenity, uninterrupted bliss. Sometimes, after an especially hard day, the idea still seems very attractive. But most of the time such a heaven feels stagnant, like the ancient Hebrew notion of Sheol, a motionless pit of nonexistence.

Nothing in this world is truly motionless, and I suspect nothing in the next world is either. We human beings think in terms of perfect ends, but I doubt that God thinks that way. I have a hunch that God has a lot more to do with tender beginnings than with efficient ends.

Neither the cosmos nor the earth, neither life nor death, is ever in perfect repose. The universe is always happening, endlessly changing, finding greater beauty, seeking deeper harmony. Life in all of creation is breaking up and gathering together, destroying and birthing. Great drifts of stellar gases coalesce and burn; giant stars implode into black holes; planetary bodies attract and repel one another. Subatomic particles—or are they waves of energy?—find and escape from one another. Atoms gather into molecules, and molecules into forms. We are a part of it all; it is in us and through us. In the words of Saint Paul, "From the beginning, the entire universe has been groaning in one great act of giving birth."[7]

The great dance of creation implies a moving toward, not an arrival. It is a continual becoming, not a final accomplishment. In it, we human beings are drawn toward greater love and ever-expanding freedom by virtue of a desire so intimate within us that it is inseparable from our very being. It is the nature of love, and therefore of our spirits, to expand, to open, to reach out, to extend and create and reunite, to be bound and liberated, to become lost in union, and to break apart painfully again in new creation. Nearly two thousand years after Paul, Rabbi Kook put it this way: "Nothing remains the same; everything is blooming, everything is ascending; everything keeps increasing in light and truth."[8]

Addiction binds and restrains our expansiveness toward freedom, whereas passion—the irrepressible energy that is our spirit—strives and yearns for release. Like gravity among the planets, addiction keeps us in orbit; it seeks stability, normality, and equilibrium. And it is *all* love. Love embraces all things, addiction as well as freedom.

In human physiology, the pull toward stability and equilibrium is called homeostasis. Homeostasis (literally, "standing in sameness") depends upon a collection of processes that serve to keep the body's internal environment stable. Areas of the brain maintain stability by regulating a host of functions, from body temperature to emotions. Claude Bernard, one of the founders of modern physiology, wrote, "All the vital mechanisms have only one object, that of preserving constant the conditions of life in the internal environment."[9]

Homeostasis is necessary for life. It provides a stable home base, a resting place from which the body can respond to the surrounding world. When something threatens this stability, we experience stress. If the body cannot maintain its interior equilibrium, it adapts to the stress by establishing a new balance, a new normality. It becomes conditioned to the stressful elements, incorporates them, and comes to depend upon them. This is precisely the way addiction happens; it is the way love becomes attached.[10]

In the service of homeostasis, addiction acts upon the human spirit like gravity upon a planetary body, seeking to hold it within a stable orbit against the planet's own centrifugal striving for the stars. In this way, our most natural addictions safeguard the essentials of life. They are part of love, but they are pure function, unadulterated efficiency, nothing but inhibition. For the spirit seeking freedom of love, as for the planet seeking the stars, the gravity of addiction is a painful price to pay for safety.

If homeostasis were the end of things, that end would surely be Sheol: stagnation and death. With no stretching, reaching, opening, or yearning to counteract our gravity, we would collapse in upon ourselves like stars becoming black holes. Often we do try to choose that option. We choose safety over freedom; we entrench ourselves in inertia. We dull and occupy ourselves so completely that we stifle our desire, anesthetize our yearning, restrict the energy of our passion. This does not remove us from the ongoing birth of creation, but it deadens us to it. And to some extent creation is subdued by our dullness; the beams of love are a little less bright. We all opt for safety on occasion, when the beams are too hard to bear. Most of us choose it more than we would like to admit. Some of us choose it continually.

It is truly a matter of choice. From love's perspective, *everything* is a matter of choice. Addiction limits our freedom of choice, but never kills it entirely. Love is too much with us, too all-encompassing to be vanquished by addiction. Love is always available, stimulating our desire no matter how much we have been hurt, encouraging us to make choices no matter how much our freedom has been restrained. Love does not permit homeostasis to be the end of things. If we so choose, whatever stability we have can be the source of endless beginnings. Our equilibrium can be gestation rather than stagnation. Homeostasis can be the place where we wake up to our yearnings, however painful, and claim them as our own. We can choose to follow our desires for more *than* what is instead of more *of* what is. We can say yes to the invitation of love and begin to open up and reach out again. Each time we say yes we upset our stability. We sacrifice our serenity. We risk our safety. We become vulnerable to being hurt. And creation shines more brightly.

Just as saying no to love does not remove us from creation, saying yes does not liberate us from addiction. But it does make a difference, not just to our own hearts, but to the whole of creation. Each human yes contributes a priceless breath of freedom to the endlessly birthing universe.

3

FREEDOM AND INTENTION

The new seers burn with the force of alignment, with the
force of *will*, which they have turned into the force of *intent*
through a life of impeccability. *Intent* is the alignment of all
the amber emanations of awareness, so it is correct to say
that total freedom means total awareness. Freedom is the
Eagle's gift to humanity.
CARLOS CASTANEDA

Let me say it again: from love's perspective, everything is a matter of choice. No matter how oppressed we may be by internal
addictions or external forces, love always ensures that some spark
of freedom of choice remains alive within us. But as we shall see,
freedom to choose is not the same thing as power to control. At
first it seems like paradox: love showers us with freedom, yet we
fall in love against our will; our loves give us glimpses of unconditional freedom, yet simultaneously we are bound by our addictions. Still more strikingly, love ensures our freedom to choose
even when we do not want it. There are plenty of times in life
when we would rather not have to make decisions; the alterna-
tives are too painful or the responsibilities too heavy. In such situations we may procrastinate or become very passive, but these
are still choices that we make. To "decide not to decide" is still a
decision. We might adopt rigid institutional values, adhere to
frozen policies, or even join cults to avoid the responsibilities

that come with making our own choices, but avoiding responsibility is also a choice. Freedom and responsibility are perfect boomerangs; they keep coming back to us no matter how or where we try to throw them away. The one thing we are never free to choose is choicelessness.

Gently but irrevocably, we are captured by freedom. It is useless to be concerned about whether to choose; the real questions are how and why we choose. Our identity is solidly rooted in our hearts' desire for love—we are made to love—but our character emerges in the choices we make about that desire. Being in love is given to us with our very lives, but the pulse of our living, our real participation in creation, is our choosing: choosing among our loves and choosing love itself.

Choosing Among Loves

If we look very closely, we can see that every choice we make is a love decision. Even the most mundane choices, like when to take out the trash or what we will eat for dessert, reflect how we are expressing our care and desire. We have so many loves—we have fallen for so many things—that they are continually conflicting with one another. We have to choose among them. I want to get the trash out, but I would rather stay in my nice warm house. I want to lose weight, but I also love ice cream. We want to help the poor, but we also want to hold on to our possessions. All our choices reflect an economy of passion: how we decide to invest ourselves in what we care about. Large and small, we make thousands of such choices every day.

Because of their sheer number, we must make most of our choices unconsciously and automatically. We rely on our conditioned habits to do this. Some habits are absolutely practical: we don't touch hot stoves; we look both ways before we cross a street; we walk through doors instead of bumping into walls.

Our habits just take care of it. Other habits are more noble. The principles of religion and society have been reinforced in us as moral and ethical habits from early childhood. Most of us refrain from taking things that don't belong to us and from attacking people who make us angry. Usually we don't even have to think about it. Our conditioning makes the decision for us.

Conditioning can be efficient or inefficient. We call efficient conditioning a talent, gift, or good personality trait. Conditioning that functions poorly we call a bad habit. I have a bad habit of cracking jokes when I am angry; it is an ingrained way of unconsciously choosing to express hostility. If our conditioning seriously defeats our deeper desires, we call it neurosis. One of my neurotic patterns is to withdraw when people express affection. When I respond from pure habit, I opt for safety rather than vulnerability.

Habits and neurotic patterns can be counteracted if we keep our decisions conscious, but it takes considerable energy and attentiveness to do so. When conditioning is deeply and rigidly entrenched, however, even diligent attention does not change it; it is stronger than our willpower. This is another way to understand addiction: making choices against our will. It happens not only in abuse of substances and behavior that is destructive but also in overwork, drivenness, perfectionism, and even in political conviction and moral righteousness. Excessive moral or political conditioning produces obsessive scrupulosity: a rigid legalism so guilt-ridden and fear-driven that free ethical choice is essentially impossible. Here the spark of freedom is very dim, and the potential for violence increases. What happens if I am severely addicted to my principles and you are just as addicted to yours, and our principles come into conflict? War.

At its best, conditioning can to some extent serve our freedom for love. In addition to providing us with a certain stability, conditioning saves us from having to consciously choose among our conflicting loves countless times each day. By making many small choices automatically, it allows us to reflect consciously upon the few decisions we consider most important. At its addicted worst, however, conditioning becomes a tyrant; it subverts our freedom for love by forcing us to bow to something other than our deepest desire. It can even force us into war. And no matter how compelled we may feel, we are still responsible for the consequences of our decisions.

To say the least, the balance between habit and freedom is delicate. We must bear full responsibility for choosing among our loves thousands of times each day, but our options are limited and often out of our control. If this were all there were to life, it would seem impossible and hardly worth it. It would be like an executive's nightmare: the kind of thing that makes ulcers. But there is more to life than choosing among loves. There is a single larger choice that can breathe freedom and spontaneity into every decision, every moment.

Choosing Love Itself

Just as falling in love is a doorway into being in love, our struggles to choose among our loves can bring us to the larger invitation of love itself. Choosing among loves is efficiency; it is how we get through our days. The invitation of love itself presents us with why. More practically, it presents us with a trustworthy, freeing grace that empowers all our daily decisions. When we are really given to the why of life, the hows begin to flow. They come less from conditioning and more from our larger, deeper desire. This is no panacea; it does not remove us from pain and struggle. On the contrary, it invites us into exquisite vulnerability. But the freedom and the meaning are immense.

Dag Hammarskjöld, United Nations Secretary General and Nobel Peace laureate, wrote these words in 1961: "I don't know

Who—or what—put the question. I don't know when it was put. I don't even remember answering. But at some moment I did answer Yes to Someone—or Something—and from that hour I was certain that existence is meaningful and that, therefore, my life, in self-surrender, had a goal."[1]

On the surface, Dag Hammarskjöld's words might indicate the yes is a one-time thing, after which everything just falls into place. Like a first kiss, our first conscious yes is precious and memorable, but it is only the beginning. Life goes on, struggles continue, and the yes is continually re-invited. Saying yes to love did not make Hammarskjöld's problems go away, nor will it ours. It will, however, give us a vision of what our problems are for, why our struggles have value beyond efficiency. No matter how our loves and fears tear at us, love itself assures us they are never the end of the world; they are always part of its eternal beginning. They are no longer hurdles we must cross before we can go on to the next thing; they are instead miraculous expressions of our living right here and now. As such, they can never overwhelm us. At times, we can even savor them. In saying yes again and again, we find a sense of our place in things, a glimpse of who we really are and how very precious each one of us is within the wondrous infinity of creation.

No matter how we may squirm to find a way out, we cannot escape being part of creation. Even suicide cannot remove our impact upon the universe; it only darkens it. Moreover, we cannot avoid being essential to it. We may lack political power and religious sophistication. We may be largely ignorant of the workings of our own minds. We may be beaten down by the circumstances of our lives and by the choiceless choices our addictions impose upon us. We even may be rejected by our friends and scorned by our colleagues. But creation would miss us if we were not here. We are significant, precious, and needed, not just for the choices we make and the actions we take, but for our very presence. The scriptures of every major religion attest to it: the love in which we exist loves us for our very being. These words from Isaiah are one example: "I have called you by name and you are mine. You are precious in my sight, and honored, and I love you."[2]

We seldom realize our preciousness. We are so busy, so occupied with many little things, that we are blind to the one great thing. Only in the pauses between things, in the brief contemplative spaces of just being, can we catch a glimpse of love itself. Even then, we often feel so unfree that we think we are unworthy of love. But the glimpses keep coming. In the momentary emptiness when an addictive need is not yet satisfied, in encountering a situation in which we do not know what to do, in finding ourselves giving or receiving a touch of tenderness for no reason at all, in the spontaneous eruption of laughter, another small space opens. The invitation is given again.

Time and again we ignore the invitations and fill the spaces immediately, dulling our consciousness with drivenness. But love continues, hoping to catch us in a willing moment. Thousands of little spaces come each day. They exist between each choice we make and the next, after each thought is completed and before the next begins, between each breath and the next, in every hunger or wanting, whenever something wakes us up to presence.

Now and then, through some mysterious interweaving of divine grace and human willingness, we see what is in the space and do not run away. We become aware of our hearts' response and are given the most wonderful experience of freedom: we are empowered to act against our habits, to move beyond our conditioning. We authentically feel a desire to be in love more consciously and more of the time, and find that we can claim the desire, own it, and act upon it. Moreover, we can see that our attempts actually make a difference. In looking for the spaces instead of avoiding them, we begin to notice more of them. We stay with them a little longer, and their tender atmosphere begins to spill over into the rest of our actions. The distinction begins to blur between choosing among loves and choosing love. We find that saying yes to love is something that can be practiced and—wonder of wonders—it works.

Saying yes to love works, but not in the way we might expect. It is the working of love, not of efficiency. It involves intention but not success or failure. It invites dedicated practice, but not achievement or competence. It is a conscious choice toward openness instead of control. Saying yes to love is not a method for breaking the chains of addiction or solving our problems, but a response to the essential goodness of love itself. It comes not from our desire to get away from something bad, but from our desire to welcome something wonderful. It is opening our hearts to a gift already given. To use Ibn al-'Arabi's terms, it is the heart embracing the reality that embraces and fills the heart.

The practice required for such willingness is very different from that which we bring to most undertakings. Normally we turn our choices into projects. We try to control things to get what we want. This is not appropriate in love. It is not even possible. The difference has to do with desire, intention, and control. It is a difference well worth understanding, because intention is the way toward love.

The Best of Intentions

Desire is wanting something, longing for some satisfaction. Intention is claiming the wanting, consciously owning it, choosing to seek satisfaction. Control is what we are able to do to make the satisfaction happen. We desire much and can intend anything we choose, but our control is limited. A child wants to fly like a bird; that is desire. She decides to try; that is intent. She tries and fails; that is control (or rather the absence of it).

The voice of efficiency would say it was a silly desire in the first place. It was impractical. But desire does not care whether something is practical or even possible. The little girl wants to fly, and the desire remains in her against all practicalities. When she actually tries to fly, practicalities take over; gravity is beyond her control. In between, gently intervening in the space between desire and control, is intention.

What happens to the little girl's intent is critical to her sense of self and identity. Having failed to fly, she may give in to the voice of efficiency. If so, she will believe her desire and intention were absurd; in the future she will squelch such immature fantasies. She will grow up believing that her longings are valuable only if they are practical. She will stifle her spirit and become a mature, well-adjusted adult.

Of all the things I dislike about psychiatry, I most abhor the notion of adjustment. What divine power ever said we should adjust ourselves to the ways of our world? Is our society so perfect, so just, so loving that it is worth adapting ourselves to? Think of the great spiritual leaders of history, and think of the most loving people you have known; were they well adjusted? Were their hearts determined by what was practical and proper? To state the point positively, what is so wrong with wanting to fly?

The natural human spirit is irrepressibly radical; it wants the unattainable, yearns for the impractical, is willing to risk the improper. But as we conform ourselves to the practicalities and proprieties of efficiency, we restrict the space between desire and control; we confine our intention to an ever-decreasing range of possibilities. The choices we make—and therefore the way we feel about ourselves—are determined less by what we long for and more by what is controllable and acceptable to the world around us. After enough of this, we lose our passion. We forget who we are.

It is imperative, not just for our individual spiritual growth but for the hope of our world, that we begin to reverse this process. We need to expand the space between desire and control, making room for that which is impractical and improper. We must give our intention room to breathe.

As a start, try to recover some of your own impossible hopes. Would you not desire peace for our world? Do you not yearn for justice and freedom for all who are oppressed? Might you not hope that suddenly, by some miracle, everyone on earth could have food and shelter? On a smaller scale, do you not long for complete love, beauty, and freedom in yourself and your relationships? Where were these desires before you called them to your consciousness? Where did you have to go to dig them up? What buried them?

Try to sit with some of your hopes for a while; just be aware of them. See if you don't begin to feel an expansion of space inside you, a certain enlarging, opening sense of possibility. Then you may hear the voice of efficiency again: "But it's impossible. It can't work. It would take a miracle. I can't do anything about it." Before long, if your mind is at all like mine, you will set your wishful thinking behind you and get on with what you think you need to do—what you can control and what is expected of you.

I will tell you one of my impossible desires. I want this world to entertain a lot more wishful thinking. I want a great many more improprieties and an endless array of impracticalities. I want to see a world in which affirmation is given to children who want to fly, no matter how often they fail. I want human intention to have all the space in the world, because intention is the most significant, the most essential, the most completely *human* thing about us. It is the place where our spirits soar. Rabbi Kook said it simply: "Intention is everything."[3]

Intention is everything because it is the only way we can truly say yes to love. Desire can only be a wanting to say yes, wistfully arising amid the confusion of countless other impulses and addictions. Control can only try to achieve results; it is immersed in the functional harshness of success and failure. Only in between, in intention, is there freedom for human authenticity.

We usually do not know what are the best, most loving of our many desires, but intention allows us to do our best to choose the best. Having chosen, we often fail, or later learn that our choice was mistaken. Still, we can know we have done our best in the choosing and in the doing, and that is our only authenticity. Even a conscious, freely chosen no to love is more true and more human than a thousand reflexive, conditioned, addicted yeses.

Even without clarity of motivation and without any sign of success, our intentional yes to love joins us to the process of creation. In the instant of our yes, we cease to be objects; we become open participants, flexible cocreators. From this ground of intention toward love, everything that is wholly and rightly human springs forth. Rabbi Kook said this highest of human intentions "embraces every thought of peace, of the battle for righteousness and equity, every assertion of wisdom, of a good and desirable order of things. Every act that perfects the world is embraced in it."[4]

Intending literally means stretching; it is a stretch of the will, reaching out for and opening up to that which we desire. We are likely to think of intention as "going for it," trying to make something happen. That is willful intention; the stretching is grasping, manipulative, forceful. Because love comes as a gift, intention toward love is different. It involves yielding as well as stretching; it is reaching out with open hands, stretching oneself open in willingness.

Intention needs space within which to express itself. It also requires two other things: human awakening and divine grace. Awakening is needed for appreciation; we cannot be intentional when we are asleep. Grace is needed for empowerment: for making intention possible in the first place, and for bringing it to fruition. With space, awakening, and grace, intention becomes our *haqqodesh*, our holy ground.[5]

Awakening

Our hearts' desire goes on no matter what; it is awake even when we sleep. But when we accept the invitation of love, our minds must awaken to our hearts; we must sense our desire and know our intent. We may not know exactly how or why we are choosing, and we most certainly do not know what we are letting ourselves in for, but we need to realize our act of opening. The yes to love, chosen with immediate awareness and full responsibility in the absence of certain knowledge, is the most free and authentic thing a human being can do. It is what the human will was created for.

It is possible to survive without self-awareness. We can delegate our choices to unconscious conditioning. Like computer programs, our homeostatic habits will adapt to changing circumstances and get us through each day. But to create, to appreciate, and to truly love, we must wake up. In immediate wakeful presence, desire is transformed from automatic impulse into heartfelt passion. Control, to the extent that it is possible, is changed from reflexive manipulation into authentic creativity. And intention has room to breathe.

Some awakenings come in flashes, but more often we awaken in stages, as if emerging from a dream. We must pass through many layers of dulled, automatic responses before we encounter the true liveliness of our hearts. I asked a young woman what she most deeply wanted. She responded immediately, "I'd like a happy home and family, security, a sense of being worthwhile." Then I asked her to sit in silence for a moment and try to be open to what desires she could really *feel,* right in the moment. After a while she looked up with tears in her eyes. "I don't know what to say. What I actually feel is that things are really okay right now. Better than okay. I don't think I want anything more than what I have at this very moment." I asked her to be still once again, to look more deeply into her present feeling, to seek any desire that might honestly be there. Softly, she said, "It's very hard to put into words. I feel really blessed, and I feel gratitude; I want to say thank you to someone. Is it God? If it is, I want to give God a hug and say thanks. And I wish people could feel this way more, could have some peace."

This woman's first reaction came from her adjusted, conditioned conceptions of herself. Her second reflection was of how things actually were for her in the present moment. Her third was the response of her heart to that reality. As she awakened to her direct perception of the immediate moment, she increasingly became aware of her authentic desire. She awoke to her desire, and it was not what she had expected.

Most of the time it works the other way round; instead of our waking up to our desire, our desires bring us to wakefulness. There is a story about a little boy who had never spoken. His parents took him to a variety of specialists, but nothing helped;

the boy remained completely silent for thirteen years. Then suddenly one morning, sitting at breakfast with his parents, he said, "The cocoa's cold." "What?" cried his astonished mother. "I said the cocoa's cold," the boy replied. His parents were themselves speechless for a moment. Then the father asked, "Why, after all these years of silence, do you now suddenly say, 'The cocoa's cold'?" "Because," the boy said, "everything was all right until now."

Physiologically, if everything were indeed all right and all our desires were satisfied, there would be no reason for speaking, or even for wakefulness. It is when we do not get what we want or when we get something we do not want that we have occasion to wake up. Neurologists have related alertness to two kinds of inner drives called motivational states. The first is homeostatic: desires for food, water, and whatever is needed for maintaining the body's stability. The second kind of motivational state is made up of creative drives like sexuality and curiosity. Together, the two motivational states are the physiologic equivalent of gravity and the spirit's desire to fly. The areas of the brain that mediate such desires are connected with centers that govern emotions such as pleasure, fear, and aggression. All these in turn are intimately connected with centers that influence wakefulness. We are awakened, brought to an increased level of perceptiveness and involvement, when such desires and emotions are stimulated.[6]

Contemplatives throughout history have understood much of this arrangement without knowing the neurology. Again and again they have described how their spirits were awakened and stirred to life by their desire for love. In the fourth century, Augustine wondered poetically how the awakening happened. "In what place then did I find You to learn of You? Thou didst breathe fragrance upon me, and I drew in my breath and do now pant for Thee: I tasted Thee, and now hunger and thirst for Thee: Thou didst touch me, and I have burned for Thy peace." John of the Cross, the sixteenth-century Carmelite friar who has been widely misinterpreted as devaluing human desire, wrote at length about how God works precisely through our desires, awakening us to incredible passion: "How gently and lovingly You wake in my heart, How tenderly You swell my heart with love." John's spiritual mother, Teresa of Avila, wrote a commentary on the Hebrew Song of Songs in which she exclaimed, "Oh, great dignity, worthy of awakening us!"[7]

Both neurological and contemplative evidence point out an essential truth about awakening: because desire awakens us, our wakefulness is always *for* something; it has a direction. We are conscious not just because our hearts are beating but because they are yearning. The very appearance of consciousness implies a purpose.

For a long time, it seems the sole purpose of awakening is to gratify specific desires. At the outset we may be awakened by something as mundane as desire for food or a dry diaper—or a warm cup of cocoa. But after its initial awakening by desire, consciousness grows. We become aware of ourselves experiencing life, and, with grace, we begin to experience the one deep desire for love that our little desires have reflected all along. Here the contemplatives go further than the neurologists; they describe a quality of consciousness existing in the absence of stimulation by homeostatic threats and creative impulses, for the love of being itself.

I think this is the awakening we experience in truly contemplative moments, moments of just being in love. Living is appreciated then without any descriptions, qualifications, or felt cause. It seems to me that this quality of just being is first encountered in childhood. I think I remember its happening when I was very little, but I cannot be sure. Or perhaps it is something all of us have always known, even before our birth. There is a sweet childhood story about why we have the little indentation above our upper lips. Before we were born, an angel whispered a secret to us. Pressing a finger to our lips, the angel said, "Don't tell." We retain the mark of the angel's finger, but we do not remember the secret. Perhaps the secret has something to do with the love that has awakened us to life.[8]

Just as we have many different loves, we have many kinds of awakenings. For example, I think our culture is so obsessed with romance because romance is such a powerful awakening. For many of us, romance has been where we have felt most alive, most energetic, most appreciative of being. Romance reminds us of free and beautiful moments of just being, moments that are themselves experiences of falling in love: falling in love with everything, with life, with being. Romance causes us to play, to dance, to become as little children. No wonder we long for it.

It is no accident that contemplatives use the language of romance to describe awakening to the great yearning of life. I have mentioned Teresa of Avila's writing a commentary on the Song of Songs. Twelve centuries earlier, Gregory of Nyssa did the same. He focused on the verse that inspired the title of this book: "I sleep, yet my heart is awake." He wrote, "Thus the soul, enjoying alone the contemplation of Being, receives the vision of God in a divine wakefulness with pure and naked intuition."[9]

The contemplatives say there is a level at which all our hearts are always saying yes to love, regardless of how dulled or preoccupied our conscious minds are and regardless of how unloving our actions may be. Saying yes to love, they maintain, represents not so much a conversion of heart as a conversion of consciousness (*shub* in Hebrew, *metanoia* in Greek) in which we awaken to turn ourselves, intend ourselves, toward that which our hearts have been wanting all along.

I find it immensely reassuring to know that deep within myself, and within all my sisters and brothers, something is always and irrevocably saying yes to love, wanting to grow into fulfillment. It helps me be more compassionate with myself and others when we fail so miserably at loving one another. It also reminds me that the journey toward greater love is not something to be instilled in people; it is already there to be tended, nurtured, and affirmed. Brother Lawrence, in a parenthetical line in *The Practice of the Presence of God,* said, "People would be very surprised if they knew what their souls said to God sometimes."[10]

Moments of contemplation, moments of realizing being in love, are times when the sporadic consciousness of our minds approaches the constant wakefulness of our hearts. It is given to us, as if someone or something has said, "Hey, wake up! Here you are! Look! Taste! See! Appreciate!" It happens in little spaces and pauses, between thoughts, between activities, between demands, between breaths.

Because we keep ourselves so dull and occupied most of the time, I am certain that these awakenings come from the power of love's grace, weaving itself through our moments and circumstances, calling us to notice the wonder of our being and empowering us, if we so choose, to intend ourselves toward our deepest desire. Grace comes as a gift. We can neither earn it nor make it happen. But grace invites us to participate; it needs our involvement.

It is time to begin asking how this participation can happen. How can we nurture our desire and encourage our intention? What can we do to embrace love's awakening presence more fully? How can we become more receptive to the gift? There is indeed much we can do; there are practices to undertake, attitudes to cultivate, realities to learn and remember. The remainder of this book is about such doings. But we must know we cannot do it alone. We can no more wake ourselves up or autonomously free our intention for love than we can conquer our addictions. This is not something to be preached, believed, or accepted on faith; it must be *known*.

For me, the first important practice was to try to do it all by myself. I had to try to master my destiny. And I had to fail, repeatedly. Without the attempt, I would never have been sure that opening to grace was not just a way to avoid my own responsibilities. I do not know how long I tried; I am only sure it was most of my life. Even still I sometimes try to do it alone, and it is not a bad thing. It lets me know my limitations, and it brings me back to deeper participation. Not everyone needs to go through this; not everyone is as stubborn as I am. But if you are in doubt, please be sure you do not accept anything I say on faith. Test it. Try in every way you can to get your life together on your own. Then, if and when you need to, turn back homeward to the source of love and grace, to the wellspring of all goodness.

The Source of Love

Grace comes from somewhere. It is given to us by someone or something. Our yes to love is a response to someone or something. I have said that efficiency is the how of life and love is the why; now we address the who. I call this someone or something God. It is a word and a name to which we all have many conditioned responses. Whether our responses make us comfortable or ill at ease, we can be sure of one thing: our understanding of God is not God. God is love, but love is not God. God is creator, but we also create. God is immanently within us, yet at the same time transcendently beyond us. God's grace is all-powerful, but we are always free to turn away from it. If love is always more than we can understand, how could we ever expect to comprehend love's source?

It would not be so difficult if we were just exploring the ethics and morality of choosing among our loves, or the psychology and neurology of falling in love. But to look at our response to being in love we simply have to confront spirituality, our direct, living connectedness with the divine. Popular psychology would like to see spirituality as the functioning of our deepest feelings and values, our most profound archetypal experience. We can indeed explain much of the love we experience for objects and other people on the basis of psychic function, but it is not possible to explain being in love this way.

Any experience of being in love confronts us with a much larger picture of our lives. We can no longer deal with love as a commodity, nor even as an energy that springs from one person's heart to another's. Being in love brings with it a recognition that we are involved in something vast, endless, beyond all distinctions and barriers. Sooner or later we will come to know that our yes is a response to our having first *been* chosen. Then the mystery of human passion deepens beyond all fathoming: Is it our desire for love or God's desire for us?[11]

Take a breath now, and look into your sense of God. When you think of God, what thoughts, images, and feelings appear in your awareness? Where have these come from? Can you trace some to your childhood, others to what you have been taught, still others to your mature experiences of life? When you reflect upon love and its source, what comes to you? Is it different from your other images of God?

Now take another breath, relax a little, and see if you can let all the images and thoughts pause for a moment. Let all your conditioned reactions come to rest. What is it like to just let God be whoever or whatever God will be, without worrying about it? Can you find a moment or two of just being there, before thinking, beyond believing or disbelieving, beneath images and associations?

I am encouraging you to let yourself be you and to let God be God. As you touch this gentle permissiveness, you may run into just a little trouble with your religious beliefs. Religious belief is a two-edged sword. It can give us a historically sound foundation and sense of community that make it more possible to relax, to trust God's goodness, and to be more fully in love. But it can also stir up reactions that complicate our simple presence and flood us with mixed messages about the nature of God. So I would suggest this: if religious belief presents some kind of problem for you, don't worry too much about it. Just try to be gently open to your own confusions and love's invitations. Don't worry whether you believe in God or not, or whether the God you believe in is the true God, or whether there might be a God other than the one you *don't* believe in. And don't worry about whether you are good enough or moral enough to be acceptable in God's eyes.

But do keep your own eyes softly attentive to the truth. Try to be as honest as you can with your experience, and as gentle as possible with yourself. Face into life as it is, into love as it comes. If the Divine is truly divine, you can risk anything for a deeper and truer consciousness of that reality. If not, you really need to take the risk of finding out. Keep coming back to your own common sense and to what you hold most dear, back to the truth of your heart. Let God be God; let the world and other people be who they are; let yourself be yourself.

This kind of letting-be is the best kind of science. Insofar as possible we must be willing to see, feel, and fully experience what is, just as it is. We cannot be sure that what we see or expe-

rience is true. In fact, given the mind tricks we play on ourselves, we can safely assume much of it is not. We can only want
the truth and try to be willing for it. When things seem uncer-
tain, we can find confidence in the truth of our desire. We can
know our yearning, our hoping, our intention. There are times
when we can be reduced to nothing other than our longing, but
it is sufficient because it is absolutely real.

At first, the idea of letting-be may seem passive. But it is an
assertive seeking of truth, and it requires two kinds of courage.
First, we must be open to things as they are, refraining from pro-
jecting our expectations onto reality. Second, we must be willing
to respond from our deepest desire, no matter how impractical,
unorthodox, or self-risking it may be. None of us will ever be
perfect in either kind of courage, and grace is necessary even to
begin. But is there really any other honest way?

Turning Toward the Source

When desire for love is felt, owned, and intended, some kind of
prayer happens. In one form or another, prayer is the beginning
and the way of being in love. If we are to say yes to love's invitation, to whom do we say it? In part, we say it to ourselves
when we claim our desire and intention. But we are also com-
mitting ourselves to receiving a gift, and thus must address the
giver. Prayer is the only way we can integrate our intention with
our dependence on grace.

Desire in itself can be prayer when it turns us toward the
source of love, turns our attention there, aligns our concern in
that direction. Of course there is no geographical direction in
which God exists in relation to us. It is an attitudinal direction,
determined by our intent. Sometimes it may seem we turn
toward the interior, toward the divine within us. At other times

we see the divine in other people, in nature, somewhere outside ourselves. And in moments of pure being, it is clear that the source of love is everywhere; our very life becomes a prayer.

Prayer can be anything from reciting words by rote, to pleading for help in desperation, to simple appreciation in the present moment. Some people have very clear-cut ideas about who God is when they pray. Others do not have a clue; their prayer is simple expression of their feelings in the hope that someone or something might hear and respond. It really does not matter. Our understandings of prayer are probably just as inaccurate as our understandings of love and of God. It is all right.

For example, I first spoke with Richard about prayer in the course of psychotherapy, during his recovery from a depression. He said he had tried to pray, but because he was not sure who God was or even if God existed, he could not begin. As we talked, it became clear to Richard that he was avoiding the act of prayer by becoming preoccupied with the nature of God. Finally he said, "I guess if God exists, then God is who God is—and I can't figure that out. And if God does not exist, well, I can't figure that out either." He decided to stop worrying about prayer and start praying. This seemed to open a floodgate within him, and he was able to pour out all kinds of feelings and concerns in prayer. His wondering about God continued, but Richard discovered a new way of responding; one day he announced, "I started praying about prayer—about God. I asked God to help me understand God more."

Jean, by contrast, was prevented from praying precisely because she did have clear ideas about God. "God is so great," she said, "and I am so small. God is so good and strong, while I am so sinful and weak. I can't even believe that God would pay attention to me." I gave her no advice but gently encouraged her to keep trying. Finally she said essentially the same thing Richard had: "I realized I'm not going to control or even really know how God will react to me—that is God's business. So I just decided to try to pray and let things sort themselves out. And really, I have to say it has been just fine."

The problem for both Richard and Jean was being overconcerned about the nature of God when what they really wanted to do was just pray to God. In both cases, their preoccupation was a reflection of wanting to maintain some control in prayer. Richard felt he could keep control if he figured out exactly who God was. Jean tried to control things by clinging to specific images of herself and God. Both people found breakthroughs only when they were willing to be more vulnerable, when they could risk letting themselves be themselves and letting God be God.

I think most people have trouble with prayer because prayer is really an act of love, and therefore demands vulnerability. As with love, the more we try to control prayer, the less prayer can happen. Yet the desire to defend and protect oneself is understandable. Prayer is where we most directly face the truth of ourselves and of the world: it is risky business indeed. When I feel the fear associated with this vulnerability, I find it reassuring to remember that the word *prayer* comes from the Latin root *precarius,* meaning to depend upon grace. From this root also comes our English word *precarious*.

Because of our fear of depending on grace, conscious intentional prayer—which should be the most honest, loving enterprise of the human heart—sometimes becomes one of the most dishonest. It seems we will do almost anything to domesticate prayer, to restrict its inherently radical nature. We try to confine it within private habits and institutional structures, going through its motions without facing its disturbing, endless freshness. We even devise hierarchies of prayer in which one form is considered more mature and sophisticated than the next. It is difficult for most of us to even think about prayer without being concerned about "doing it right" or comparing our prayer to someone else's.

It is for this reason that I have suggested you not be worried about trying to define who you are or who God is, and now I further encourage you not to be concerned about your form or style of prayer. Seek only honesty and truth, come to your best sense of your desire, and just be there as you are, with God as God may be. Feel free to experiment. You need not conform yourself to any prescribed regimens or images of what good prayer should look like. At the same time, if structured forms of prayer arise that seem natural to you, you need not restrain them. Allow as much openness to radical freshness as you can, yet be willing to give yourself to ritual or routine if that is what seems most authentic.

Take another few minutes now to reflect on your own experience of prayer. When you try to pray, what do you do? Do you sit up straight, kneel, close your eyes, bow your head, put your hands in a special position, try to focus your mind in some way? If you have any such routines of prayer, think about them a little. Do they seem authentically helpful, or are some of them empty habits or dutiful obligations? Do you adopt any ritualized attitudes about yourself in prayer? Do you censor certain thoughts or emotions? Can you be angry with God? Can you laugh and be silly in prayer? Are there places in your life where you would never think of turning to God?

Now look back over your life with an eye for times when prayer has just happened, naturally and spontaneously. You may not have known it as prayer at the time, but look for hints of immediacy in the present moment, honesty of desire, some kind of reaching toward the source. You may find some clues here, some ways of natural, uncontrived prayer that you might want to claim and cultivate.

If there is any "right" way of praying, it is that most simple and yet elusive one: to simply be yourself. A Quaker woman once told me she was looking for "unexpurgated prayer." I believe that is what God is hoping for also: our being with God consciously just as we are with no censorship, no cleaning up our act, no posturing or posing—just being real.

You might be concerned about the degree of openness I am advocating here. Do we not need to be cautious about deluding ourselves and just doing whatever feels good? Do we not risk privatism or quietism with such an emphasis on personal authenticity? Isn't it important to distinguish whether we are opening ourselves to the grace of God or to some darker power?

If you are trying to be honest and true with yourself and God, you will become aware of such concerns from time to time, and it would be artificial not to respond to them. You may find you need some critical reflection with others, support from a community of faith, or some modification of your practice of prayer. The important thing is not to let such worries take you away from prayer. Take them into prayer instead.

But in all truth I am not very worried about such distortions, and I don't think you need be either. We all make mistakes; we always will. But God is good, and if we fuss too much about how we might be distorting prayer or how the devil might be deluding us, we will not get around to praying—which is our only real means of seeking guidance and protection anyway! I assure you my ease is not naive. I am not propounding a simplistic duality between good and evil, nor am I discounting the real, living presence of darkness. I studied and practiced psychiatry for a quarter of a century; I know how the human mind can fool itself and how selfishness can masquerade as righteousness. I worked in a prison with people convicted of repeated crimes of physical violence, and I was in the military for the majority of the Vietnam war, so I have no doubt that evil exists and that we humans are capable of absolute destructiveness. And I have spent enough time in silence to know that my own impulses, perceptions, and addictions often lead me astray. I believe in sin, not only as making mistakes or being compelled by addiction, but also as hard, calculated meanness.

But I have also prayed. My life of prayer has always been stumbling and fitful, but it has convinced me of some basic truths. We are in love. God is absolutely and always present, intimately active and involved with us, and endlessly good. As God's creations, we bear an essential part of God's own goodness in our hearts that can never be removed, no matter how selfish, prejudiced, and vindictive we may be, no matter what we have done or what has been done to us. And when we say yes to love, or try to say yes, or even just honestly desire to try to say yes, love is as victorious in that moment as it is in all of cosmic time. Bought at the price of God's own suffering, it is a victory that is always happening and always yet to come, always beginning yet never wavering for an instant. The victory only brightens by taking place within a broken and suffering world, in ways that cause us to join the suffering rather than escape it. The victory becomes more glorious, more triumphant with each human yes, and with every deepening of a yes already said.

The great spiritual leaders of our world have not preached fear and paranoia. They have said that we can trust divine goodness, that we can risk vulnerability if our intent is toward love. It is not blind faith, but an open-eyed willingness to see things as they are—the good and the bad—and in the seeing to trust and risk that grace will be given. You can give your time to making sure you do things right, and then wonder why you are so self-preoc-cupied. You can spend your energy trying to avoid the devil, who I am certain would be pleased to get so much of your attention. Or you can give yourself to seeking the love and light of God, who would be absolutely delighted. You can fear hell or desire heaven. You choose.

When you have concerns about praying, pray about them. Pray about prayer. Ask the source of love to help you pray, to protect you, to show you your way, to make it possible. Prayer just happens as part of being in love. It is not that it should or ought to happen; it just does. And it happens in your heart more often and more steadily than you will ever know.

Ironically, I have said these many words about prayer in the hope that you will not overcomplicate the process. Desire, once claimed, becomes intention. Intention, given the grace not to derail itself into superstitious control, becomes a willing, honest turning toward the source of love. In and through that love, all you need is already given. You do not need to learn another single thing. Only allow your spirit to fly.

4

THE CONSECRATION OF HOPE

I it am, the Might and the Goodness of the Fatherhood;
I it am, the Wisdom of the Motherhood;
I it am, the Light and the Grace that is all blessed Love.
I am that maketh thee to love.
JULIAN OF NORWICH

We have so vastly overcomplicated our lives that the homeward journey toward natural simplicity is tortuous. It is the kind of thing myths are made of; we go off seeking our treasure in foreign lands, finally to discover that what we sought was right here and now—at home—all along. The journey is necessary for most of us. It is our stumbling way of claiming our desire for love and consciously intending to follow it. It is indeed a sacred journey, a pilgrimage home. The journey is our act of consecration: the way we dedicate ourselves to the source of love.

Consecration is defined as dedication to a divinity. The word comes from the Latin roots *com*, "with," and *sacer*, "sacred." It implies intentionally participating with the divine. We can be dedicated to anything: to a task, a cause, a nation. But we can be consecrated only to God.

Consecration means consciously participating in love, intentionally opening ourselves to accept the divinely given gift. It requires that we trust more in grace than in our personal capabilities. It calls for an attitude of willingness, a giving of ourselves to a power greater than our own. To say yes to love, we must trust enough or risk enough to be willing to *enter* love. We must desire to join its essential liveliness.[1]

There are many specific nuances to consecration that we will need to explore, but first try a brief exercise. Relax a little right now, and be attentive to your breathing. Notice your breath coming in and going out. Dedicate yourself to being aware of your breath in each moment. Follow it with your attention from the beginning of each inhalation, when your chest starts to expand and you can feel the air coming into your nose or mouth, through the little pause when the inhalation stops and exhalation starts, to the last gentle expression of air at the end of exhaling. Take time to follow several breaths this way.

Now think about what happened. As you became aware of your breath you probably took control of it. Just noticing your breathing caused you to "do" it to some extent. Try it again if you need to, and notice how automatically you start to alter the natural rhythm of your breathing. Your breath, like love, is something that goes on all the time by itself. It happens naturally. Yet, when you become aware of it, you almost cannot help but take it over with your own will and control.

This is the way we are with most intentions. Consciously claiming the desire to simply be in or with something almost compels us to try to control it. We are so conditioned to associate intention with control that it happens like a reflex. It is as if we suddenly do not trust the process that had been going on perfectly by itself before we noticed it.

Now do the exercise again, only this time surround your attempt with consecration. In whatever way seems most authentic and uncontrived to you, remind yourself that your breath, your life, your being, is *given* to you. It is dependable. You can let it be, trust it, join it, give yourself to it. If religious language is comfortable for you, you might think of the Spirit of God breathing you. If not, simply trust the divinely given nature through which your breath happens. If even that feels too mystical at the moment, just trust your own physiology. But keep open to the wonder of this body of yours, the marvel of where it comes from, and the immense mystery of why it exists at all. Risk that the mystery of your being is trustworthy.

Spend some time with this practice, noticing how deepening your attitude of trust enables you to relax and give yourself more completely and how this in turn allows your breath to be more natural. Your awareness will still probably continue to influence your breathing somewhat, but you can sense yourself gentling into more participation than control, more appreciation than management. Experiment with the exercise; come back to it from time to time. See how it changes with your moods and energy levels. See if your trust in the natural process of your breathing deepens over time, so that you have less need for control.

Of all the intentional practices I have tried in my own pilgrimage, this little exercise with the breath has been the most valuable from a practical standpoint. It has given me both an appreciation of the trusting nature of willingness and an opportunity to unlearn some of my automatic attempts to control things. I did it quite regularly for about six months; now, I can easily follow my breath without manipulating it. What a strange little achievement (it is not something I mention to my next-door neighbors), but it opened a door into deeper prayer and being for me.

There are three potential values in this exercise. First, it can help you explore the subtle differences between simple intention and sacred consecration. Second, it can be a real practice of consecration. Repeating the exercise will help you develop a softer, more participative attitude with your breath, which can spill over into other areas of your experience. You will find it easier, for example, to allow thoughts and feelings to come and go without having to manage them. Hopefully, it will help you become more comfortable with just being in love.

The third value of the practice lies in its symbolism. Breath has always been the primary archetypal symbol of spirit, the power of life. In Hebrew, Latin, Greek, Sanskrit, and a number of other languages, the words for spirit and breath are identical. Breath not only signifies our physical life; it also connects us intimately with every other living thing on earth. The air we all breathe is the same, surrounding us and endlessly circulating among us.

Spirit, life, and love: these are the realities our breath represents. In the physiology of breathing, we put energy into the inhalation. The diaphragm muscle contracts; the chest and abdomen expand. This creates a space within us, and atmospheric pressure causes air to flow into our lungs. The exhalation is a relaxation of our respiratory muscles, giving the air back into the atmosphere, to intermingle with the breath of all other creatures. As in love, as soon as we create the necessary space, we are joined to the life of the world.

Self-awareness Without Self-consciousness

In being aware of your breathing, you may have noticed not only the tendency to take control but a certain awkwardness as well. Try being aware of walking when you walk, or of talking when you talk; the same thing is likely to happen. Actions that normally flow smoothly without our direct awareness become contrived and hesitant when we watch them closely.

In the Shalem Institute's program for spiritual guides, one of the problems participants must face is how to look closely at their own prayerfulness without changing its natural flow. I always tell them the story of the ant and the centipede. One day an ant was busy working when a centipede walked by. The ant stopped to marvel at the way the centipede moved. "I have to ask you," said the ant, "how do you manage to keep all those legs going without getting them all tangled up?" The centipede stopped to think about it and never moved again.

The problem surfaces any time we examine our natural activity. Suddenly we are not quite sure how to proceed; we feel awkward and ill at ease. Sometimes, like the centipede, we become so stiff and stilted we are essentially paralyzed. If it is difficult with breathing, it is even more so with something as intimate and subtle as our desire for love.

The problem, as I have indicated, is our conditioned association between awareness and control. We reflexively try to manage everything we pay close attention to. If we do not actively manipulate it, we will at least judge it or make some mental comment about it. Is it good or bad, safe or dangerous, acceptable or improper? This compulsion is another example of addiction to efficiency; the capacity to evaluate and manipulate is a wonderful gift—if only we didn't always *have* to do it.

The saddest result of this compulsion is that we seek relief from it through dulling ourselves. When we tire of the endless judgments and management that we assume are necessary for life and work, we seek rest by running away from self-awareness. We lose ourselves in so-called recreation, when what we really long for is simply being ourselves. We choose dullness and entrancement because self-awareness implies work. It does not occur to us that we might just be in simple, wakeful presence without having to work at it. This is why so few of us nowadays can sit on our porch of an evening, just appreciating being there.

Like all addictions, this one can be broken with grace and consecration. It is not easy, and it does take practice. But it can happen. In fact, it *must* happen if we truly want to expand our moments of being in love and to live more of our life in immediate, participative presence. The breath exercise can help a lot. So can the simple experience of space I have encouraged you to find in your life. Just sit for a while without any special agenda, and see if you can let thoughts and feelings come and go naturally.

You will find it easier, I think, if you simply open your awareness to the immediate situation instead of focusing too intensely on yourself. Come into the moment; become aware not only of yourself but also of other people and the sights and sounds around you. At first this may feel distracting, as if you have to attend to everything and process it somehow. There is so much going on. But ease up. Be gentle.

You can bring immediate awareness to all kinds of activities. Experiment with it. Watch your hands move as you wash the dishes or work in the garden. Walking down the sidewalk, bring it to mind: "Here I am, walking down the sidewalk." If this makes your walking become somewhat jerky, keep practicing—consecrate, trust, relax—until walking consciously becomes just as fluid and easy as walking unconsciously. Ask yourself the ant's question: "How do these feet and legs do what they do? How marvelous!" What had been judgment and control can, with a little space and grace, become appreciation and wonder.

As you become more comfortable with immediate self-awareness, try it with more difficult actions such as writing or talking. Notice how your hands move as you write, and bring your attention into the present moment as you speak. Speaking used to be a very centipedelike experience for me. It was humbling. I am a professional speaker; I give lectures, teach classes, lead groups, and spend hours in counseling. I found that when I brought immediate attention to the act of talking, my words became stiff and my speech faltering. This meant, of course, that I was used to talking unmindfully. When I opened my mouth, my awareness would go into a cloud. In years past, I joked about people whose minds disappeared when they started to speak, but no more. I have been one of them, and I know what it's like. Now, however, with a little practice and a lot of grace, I can speak smoothly with full, immediate consciousness.

The Sacrament of the Present Moment

What good is it that I have solved the centipede's problem and can now walk and talk and work with immediate awareness? Does it bring me any closer to realizing the presence of God? Does it help me be in love?

The answer is yes—unequivocally. The mindfulness itself is relative. At times it does help my efficiency, because when I do something mindfully I really do it; my mind is not off somewhere involved in something else. But that is pure function and of very secondary value. The great goodness of immediate awareness is that it forms the only foundation upon which true consecration can happen. To claim my desire for love most fully, I must *feel* that desire, right here and now in the midst of my daily activities. To say yes to love, I need to form my intention, with authentic presence in this real moment. To consecrate my intention, I must consciously be involved with God—realize that God is involved with all of us—right here and right now. This can happen fully only with immediate, present-centered awareness.

I can tell you how it happens for me. Sometimes, noticing the moment, I simply remember God. The remembrance does not take me out of the moment, because God is *in* the moment. It is what Brother Lawrence called the little interior glance, just a simple recognition of divine presence whenever immediate awareness happens. At other times, it is more a feeling than a thought. I sense my yearning physically. I do not stop to comment about it or, usually, even to savor it. My desire for love is nearly always perceivable as part of the moment, and recognizing its presence *is* my consecration. At still other times, when I am terribly caught up in activity or strife, I feel distant from both God and my own desire. Then I can only recall my desire to desire. And, because it is what is real in that moment, it is sufficient. Thus consecration is possible whenever immediate awareness happens. The two become one. The more frequent the awareness, the more constant the consecration.

You will need to find the ways of immediate consecration that are authentic for you; they may or may not be like mine. You will find them only by first waking up to the here and now. In the beginning, you may feel there is too much to contend with in the moment. Give it time, ask God for the grace and guidance to help you find your way, and keep trying. Remember that it is not a matter of success or failure. Every attempt you make, however stumbling, is an expression of your care, which is to say, your love.

There is nothing new here. For centuries, people seeking greater realization of love have first sought immediate, wakeful presence as the practical foundation of their intention. Standing awake in the here and now, consecrating their desire in the sacrament of the present moment, they have claimed their yearning for love. Awakening from his dream, Jacob said, "Surely the Lord is in this place and I did not know it." "Take no thought of the morrow," said Jesus, "Stay awake, praying constantly." In the church of the early fifth century, Augustine's prayer echoed Jacob's realization: "Too late loved I Thee, O Thou Beauty of ancient days, yet ever new! Too late I loved Thee! And behold, You were within, and I apart." Speaking of holy wisdom, Augustine said "to 'have been' and 'hereafter to be' are not in her, but only 'to be', for she is eternal." In 1667,

Brother Lawrence told his superior that "we need only to know God intimately present in us, to address ourselves to God at every moment." The phrase "sacrament of the present moment," comes from the translated writings of Jean-Pierre de Caussade, a French Jesuit priest of the early eighteenth century. Emphatically describing his experience of faith, he said that everyone could be a saint by simple responsiveness to God's presence in each moment: "There are no moments which are not filled with God's infinite holiness so that there are none we should not honour." In the twentieth century, Thomas Kelly proclaimed a Quaker's perspective on what he called "The Eternal Now": "Continually renewed immediacy, not receding memory of the Divine Touch, lies at the base of religious living." Thich Nhat Hanh, the modern Vietnamese Zen master and peacemaker, uses the phrases "miracle of mindfulness" and "present moment wonderful moment."[2]

Continually renewed immediacy in the present wonderful moment: I can think of no better description. Just repeat the words to yourself; it is a homecoming. There is more to it than a state of mind or consciousness. Immediate awareness, by means of consecration, has a purpose. Jesus' words about taking no thought of tomorrow occurred in the context of seeking God first, before all other concerns. His cautions about wakefulness and prayer spoke of steadfastness in the service of love. Augustine's "too late" referred to direct realization of God's presence. The present moment was a sacrament to de Caussade because it manifests God's will: "an immense ocean which the heart only fathoms in so far as it overflows with faith, trust, and love." Brother Lawrence sought the present moment in order to practice the presence of God. Thomas Kelly's continually renewed immediacy was his avenue toward world justice. "Social concern is the dynamic Life of God at work in the world, made special and emphatic and unique, particularized in each individual and group who is sensitive and tender in the leading-strings of love." Thich Nhat Hanh's mindfulness is in the service of "being peace."[3]

Prayerful Presence, Powerful Presence

If we were seeking immediate presence for the sake of improving our efficiency in life, it would be good popular psychology, nothing more. But consecration requires a reason beyond service of self; love has a larger purpose.

For over a decade, I have collected observations of the physical effects of contemplative practices. Let me describe just three. First, people who practice this kind of discipline over periods of years report an expansion of perception. No longer are they simply aware of this or that, but instead they experience a more panoramic, all-inclusive awareness. It is like what athletes and artists sometimes describe at moments of peak performance. A football player said, "When I see the ball coming toward me, everything opens up. I am aware not just of the ball but of everything: the other people on the field, the feel of the wind, the sound of the crowd. I can even sense the beating of my heart and the shape of the clouds in the sky."

Most of us would be troubled by so much information hitting us all at once, but a second effect of contemplative practice is a natural, flowing responsiveness that deals with the situation of the moment spontaneously and incisively. It is something often experienced briefly in crisis. An emergency room nurse described her reaction after a major earthquake. "There were scores of injured people. People were screaming, sirens screeching. I was worried about my family. Yet somehow I just responded. Something in me knew where to go, what to do. I did everything necessary. I was not in a daze. I can still vividly recall each sight, sound, and smell." With contemplative experience, such immediate and accurate responsiveness becomes more natural.

A third effect of contemplative practice is self-knowledge. Immediate present awareness means noticing not only what is around oneself, but what is within as well. It may not be a pleasant process, because it involves facing painful and uncomplimentary aspects of oneself. But over time, one gains a much more realistic appraisal of one's strengths and weaknesses. Psychoanalysts would say there is less repression. More of what had been unconscious has become conscious.[4]

Think for a moment about the impact of these three effects: expanded perception, enhanced responsiveness, and greater self-knowledge. A person who combines these qualities is a person of considerable efficiency. There is power here. But is there love? The *ninja* of feudal Japan trained in contemplative practices precisely to develop such capacities, and used them to become some of the most efficient assassins the world has known.

There is nothing inherent in any spiritual practice that guarantees it will be used for good and not for ill. Spiritual things can be used for very unloving purposes. I have been struck with how frequently we use religion to be mean to each other. An extreme example is the Christian Crusade or the Islamic *jihad* in which infidels are killed for Christ or Allah. Simply consider the churchly arrogance with which we scorn those who challenge or defy our beliefs.

It has probably always happened. I recall it first with a religious club some of my childhood friends formed. I don't remember what the club was exactly, but I do remember that they would not let me join. I wasn't good enough. Decades later, during the sensitivity training fad, it seemed everyone around me had suddenly got in touch with their feelings. Religious people were no exception. I heard two members of a congregation talking about a third. "He's all in his head, poor fellow, always head-tripping." They were using the jargon to be mean. I still cringe when someone comes close to my face and says, "I feel I have to share my feelings with you." Not long after sensitivity training, the charismatic renewal movement became popular in many churches. I recall a woman coming to me in tears saying, "I tried to speak in tongues, I really tried. They say I don't have enough faith." Then came personality typing: "She's an ESTJ; what can you expect?" or "Well, I'm a 2 on the Enneagram, and I'm not going to take care of you!" More recently, meanness has happened in Twelve-Step ways, as everyone wants to be recovering from something. At a committee meeting, two people walked out because of a conflict with a third person. "We are not going to be codependent with you," they said. "You'll just have to handle things on your own." Like all good things in life, recovery can be used to get our own way if we just twist it a little.

The selfish use of religion, spirituality, and now psychospirituality is nothing new. I have done it myself. Much of the time, spiritual selfishness happens in spite of our best intentions. Our hearts are in the right place; we are seeking love, connectedness, healing, and wholeness. But we play tricks on ourselves, unconsciously becoming prideful and manipulative. The power of grace is essential to deliver us from this self-treachery. Because we distort our own perceptions, we cannot do it ourselves. We can, however, reach out for grace in consecrating our intent. To use the language of Twelve-Step programs, we must keep honestly admitting again and again our powerlessness to control things ourselves, and consciously seek the grace of God's higher power.[5]

Mixed Motivations

Our motivations are seldom, if ever, completely pure. We might claim and authentically feel that our basic desire is to be in love whatever the cost, but other motivations will take precedence many times each day. We find ourselves more interested in solving our problems or gaining peace of mind than wanting to be in love. Then we may hope to kill two birds with one stone; being in love, we hope, will also solve our problems.

As an example, many people in Twelve-Step and other healing programs develop a strong sense of spirituality. In the beginning, God is the savior to whom they must surrender in admitting their powerlessness over addiction. The emphasis on God's saving power is very orthodox, but is it serving love or efficiency? In many cases, recovery becomes an idol; it is the most important thing in life, and God is only a power source for grace, like a cosmic outlet we must plug ourselves into to achieve the ends we want. This is the God of foxholes, of despair, the God whose only purpose is to rescue us.

There is certainly nothing wrong with seeing God as savior; it is just that God is and wants to be so much more than that. Many of us come to an awareness of our desire for love through our need for some kind of healing or recovery. I would never have reclaimed my own search for the divine had I not been driven to it by desperation. But this can only be the beginning of authentic spiritual life. As we grow in love, the source of love becomes more important than anything. Everything, health and recovery included, becomes relative and is even put at risk.

Although the holy One continues to be deliverer and sustainer, love calls us beyond using God to satisfy our needs, to heal us, to get us out of trouble, or to enhance our efficiency. Love calls us to gratitude, relinquishment, celebration, service, play, praise, companionship, intimacy, communion, and always to deeper yearning. In other words, love calls us to love.[6]

Honesty

No matter how mature we are, we can always deceive ourselves. The best we can do on our own is try to be honest. For the rest, we are dependent on grace. Gently and prayerfully, we need to be asking ourselves and God some questions. Are we seeking love primarily to enhance our efficiency, overcome addictions, solve problems, or be freed from depression or anxiety? Or are we responding instead to a deeper desire—the desire for love regardless of how we feel or how functional we are? A judgmental attitude is not called for here; there is nothing to be gained by self-flagellation. But we do need to be as clear as possible about what we are after. Consecration demands as much honesty as we can muster.

We may quite legitimately start out with only the desire to solve our problems, but if we are honest we will sense love catching us up in its larger net. As we are increasingly caught by love, our usual standards of efficiency will take a beating. I have found, for example, that I must work a little less in order to even begin to appreciate the work I do. There are points where I may need to become a little less job-efficient if I want to be more loving. I find also that in order to be more open to love in human relationships, I must neither try to possess nor try to control other persons, and I must even refrain from strategizing my behavior with them.

From my habitual understandings of how to deal with people, this is inefficient indeed. It created considerable conflict with the standard practice of the profession for which I was trained; I never could figure out how to fit love into a treatment plan or a set of behavioral objectives. In all such cases, I find myself trying to wangle a deal. I want to have my cake and eat it too. Why can't I be a perfectly efficient and perfectly loving psychiatrist (or teacher, administrator, pastor, or homemaker) at the same time? The answer is simple if we are honest; we can't do it because vocational standards of efficiency are set by the culture around us, and they are not the standards of love.

Honesty also means admitting the deals I try to make, the compromises I settle for. I do not always seek love. Too much of the time my agenda is far from it. But I do try to have the courage to admit what it is I seek. Honesty is the meeting ground, and sometimes the battleground, between efficiency and love. It is the foundation of consecration.

When you try to take an honest look at your motivations, begin by asking yourself some good, hard efficiency questions. Why go through all this? What is in it for me? What do I hope to achieve? Like all questions of efficiency, these have a certain harsh way of looking for ends and goals. But they are not bad questions; they help you confront the world in which you live. Don't try to justify or explain yourself; it won't work. But listen clearly to your mind and heart responding. Now ask yourself the questions of love, the questions that have to do with beginnings. What draws me? Who calls me? What is my deepest desire? What/Who is stirring my spirit and making me feel most alive? Listen again to your mind and heart responding.

As the great poet Rainer Maria Rilke said, the truly deep questions of life are to be lived, not answered. Seeking authentic desire in the heart is not like trying to grasp and examine some objective thing. It is more a gentle immersion of oneself in one's very real, immediate being. The twentieth-century monk and author Thomas Merton said, "Love is not a problem, not an answer to a question. Love knows no question. It is the ground of all, and questions arise only insofar as we are divided, absent, estranged, alienated from that ground."[7]

In summary, honesty provides a ground for consecration in two ways. First, a hard look at efficiency acknowledges the mixed nature of our motivations and lets us know something of the conflict we are likely to encounter with the world. Second, through a deep appreciation of our love, honesty permits us to affirm our longings and offer them to God in hope.

Expectation and Hope

Efficiency breeds expectation; love nurtures hope. Can you tell the difference? In the abstract, hope is a wish for something; expectation is assuming it is actually going to happen. Expectations can be very efficient if they are based on real experience. It is useful to expect that two and two will make four, or to expect that the sun will come up tomorrow. But false expectations only breed trouble.

By contrast, there is no such thing as false hope. Hope deepens our love precisely because it does not have to be bound by experience. A child who has always gone hungry cannot expect the next meal to be full but surely and rightly can hope. Because hope always admits its uncertainty, it can be disappointed but never killed. It is always open-ended.

Expectation refuses to permit wonderings or doubt, and so it is closed off, final and frozen. When an expectation is not met, it dies. Sometimes, with grace, hope is born from the rubble of dashed expectations. More often, the death is simply denied, reality is ignored, and another expectation—just as rigid and just as impossible—is forged. Without some birth of hope, each remanufactured expectation is covered with a thicker coat of cynicism and paranoia. Expectation is brittle and can only be shored up by delusion, but hope is soft and willing to suffer pain.

In real-life situations, expectation can masquerade as hope. A young man found himself repeatedly hurt in his relationships with women. His psychologist told him that he was continually setting up relationships that would fail because he was looking for the perfect mother he never had. At the beginning of each such relationship, the man felt what he thought was hope. But underneath was an expectation, a demand that the relationship be exactly what he wanted.

The wife of an abusive alcoholic kept "hoping" her husband would stop drinking and beating her. But she took no action against him because what she called hope was really an expectation that he would change. She kept convincing herself, against all evidence, that it just would not happen again. But of course it did, repeatedly.

In both cases, false expectations had to be relinquished and true hopes claimed. The young man found healing when he learned that he could only hope for the mothering he desired, but not expect it. This allowed him to interact with women in a real, dynamic way. The woman found freedom when she realized her husband's behavior was going to continue in spite of her expectations. This allowed her to intervene in ways that were realistically helpful for both herself and her husband. She continued to hope that he would change, and eventually, because she took action, he did.

Hope is flexible, willing to change or even to be given up if need be. But as the above cases demonstrate, true hope is not at all passive. Its very flexibility allows hope to be alive and active in response to all situations. It is expectation that is truly passive, frozen into paralysis or compulsive repetition. Once an expectation becomes solid, you cannot give it up. It digs into your spiritual skin like a tick, infesting your attitudes and behavior. Given the slightest opportunity, expectation will become addiction.

You can sense the entrenching quality of expectation by its ritualization, its unwillingness to encounter and be involved with life as it is, its rigid clinging to unreal belief. Compulsive gamblers do not simply hope to win; they expect it. I am like that with fishing. To put it kindly, I am an avid fisherman. When I tell this to spiritual people, they often say something like, "How nice. You can spend such quiet time there by the water, just enjoying creation." I wish it were true, but I am addicted to fishing. I expect to catch fish. I expect to catch big fish. I expect to catch a lot of big fish. It makes no difference that I very rarely catch a big fish and never in my life have caught a lot of big fish. I expect it anyway. So my fishing is rigid, ritualized, and as superstitious as a sorcerer's rite. Each cast will net the big one. I focus on the line as it enters the water with a concentration I once would have been proud of if I could have done it in prayer. I do not see the trees and the sky, or if I see them, they only speak to me of places where fish hide and of weather that affects their biting.

Sometimes when honesty catches me I think about hope and fishing. You know what? If I am really honest, I almost hope I won't catch anything. I don't really want to cause the pain. I honestly think I'd give up fishing altogether if I could honor my hope instead of obey my expectations. But I can't, or I don't want to. It's an addiction all right. Since it is impossible for me to simply hope to catch a fish—I have given up hope for that—I can sometimes hope to enjoy the water and the trees, to really involve myself with the natural beauty of the lake. For this, though, I must leave my fishing tackle at home.

Expectation, like efficiency, looks at the ends of things, for goals and accomplishments. Hope, like love, looks to the beginnings, for promptings, longings, urgings. A religious sister who lives most of her life as a contemplative hermit visited the Shalem office not long ago. We asked her about her life and travels. "Most of what I do," she said, "is just follow my urges. I think I would tell people: if you want to find God, just follow your urges." Her eyes twinkled as she said this, as if she knew how radical it might sound in some religious circles. We did not need to ask her, for we knew that urges to her were not whims and fancies. She meant real desire. Real desire, the deeper prompting of our hearts, is where hope finds its continual beginning.

In building the foundations of consecration, immediacy helps us be honest. Honesty helps us sift through our mixed motivations and chip through our expectations to find our real desire. Desire births hope, and it is our hope that we offer for grace in consecration. In some African and Native American tribes, the ritual for blessing a newborn baby involves a parent holding the infant up to the sky. It is something like that, I think, when we embrace our hope and lift it in consecration.

Fantasy

As intention is the space between desire and control, and honesty is the meeting ground or battleground between love and efficiency, fantasy is the borderland between hope and expectation. Fantasy includes some of the wishful qualities of hope and some of the controlling qualities of expectation. The classical psychological understanding is that fantasy is a way of handling things when reality fails to meet our expectations. If it is overdone, fantasy can be an escape from reality. The old one-liner is that neurotics build castles in the sky, psychotics live in them, and psychiatrists collect the rent.

But fantasy can be more than escape. It can be a way of self-exploration, a form of play, a vehicle for creativity, even a way of praying. Like anything else, fantasizing can become addictive. Nearly everyone has some kind of obsessive fantasy: sexual, fearful, or wishful. When fantasies are compelled, they fill up creative space and preoccupy us when we want to do other things. Seriously obsessive fantasies need to be dealt with as any debilitating addiction is, with committed, surrendered simplicity.

But the fact that fantasies can become addictions does not mean we should avoid them. Food, sexuality, intimacy, and many other good things can become addictions, but if we tried to exclude them from our lives we would be seriously crippled. The exploring, envisioning, playful, and prayerful possibilities of fantasy have clear, worthwhile potential. I even think it's fine to use fantasy as an escape from reality now and then. Compared to most of the other things we do to escape, fantasy seems downright noble.

If we look at fantasy in terms of consecration, a subtle discrimination must be made. We begin with our heart's honest desire, claiming it and turning toward God in hope. Then we might begin to fantasize what things would be like if our hope were fulfilled. We may project our hopes into expectations, trying to predetermine the form that grace might take. We do not have to go much further than this to close ourselves off to the radical surprises of love.

I remember a conflict with a coworker; we had misunderstood each other and were both hurt and angry. I had enough presence of mind (or was it grace?) to pause, reflect, and pray a little about the situation. My anger eased quickly and was replaced by a strong desire for reconciliation. If I had just let that be my hope, there would have been no problem. But instead my mind went on to imagine how the reconciliation might happen. I pictured my coworker and I taking a walk together, talking through our disagreement, making up and laughing about our previous trouble. Even that fantasy would have been beautiful and probably helpful if I could have let it be. It could have been my prayer: "See, God, this is how I really hope it could be." Or in my more usual style of prayer: "If you'd like my opinion, God, this is the way You should do it."

But I pushed the fantasy beyond hope into expectation. I figured I could make it happen. I approached my colleague and asked her if she'd like to take a walk and talk things over. She said no! She felt I was pushing her, not giving her enough space. We both wound up more angry than before.

The error I made is an extremely common one, especially for praying people. We want to do the right thing. We know enough to look to God for help and guidance. But we keep rushing ahead of grace. Maybe it is our need to control things, or maybe it is missionary zeal, but something grabs us out of the present moment and projects us into the future, where we try to make things fit our images of love. It does not matter whether the images come in willing prayer or from willful strategy; when we take on the job of making them work, we have left God's grace behind.

No matter how noble a fantasy may be, when we grasp it and willfully try to make it happen we are not being fair to ourselves, to God, or to whatever poor souls we may think we're trying to help. God just doesn't work that way. God does not give us our mission orders for the day and then leave us to carry them out on our own. I know this is a popular conception of God, but it is neither a loving conception nor one that is grounded in scripture or tradition. It is another efficiency model. Most often, I think, it is a way of trying to be willful and religious at the same time. "Just show me what to do, God, and then *I* will go out and do a good job for you." God lets us play such games, but only because of love. And I have to say I think it hurts God when religious people cannot trust God's presence with them all the time. We are more to God than servants.[8]

Surely we don't feel God's presence with us all the time. But just because you don't feel your hair growing doesn't mean you're bald. (If you are bald, please think of another metaphor.) There is a place for real prophetic insights to happen in prayer, in fantasy, in dreams, or just out of the blue. But there is no place for packing up the insights and running away from God with them. God is here now whether we sense it or not. We are here now. The situation is here now. The insight is here now. We can plan for the future, hope, pray, fantasize, and even strategize—all right here and now. And we must act right here and now where grace is. Sometimes fantasy can be a means of consecration, but only to the extent that it helps us cherish our hope and offer it more directly to the here and now of God.

Discretion

Consecration can become very lonely. As I have said, it takes us away from the efficiency orientations of society, away from our normal habits of interacting with people, away from our usual expectations of ourselves and the expectations others have of us. This would be no problem—it would be a relief—if only we could explain ourselves to those around us. But it does not work. We are continually forced back into nothing but our desire: "I just want to." And most of the people around us will not understand. Some discretion is called for.

I am reminded of an old Sufi story about the crazy-holy man Nasrudin. He was called upon to judge the complaint of one neighbor against another. After the prosecution made its case, Nasrudin said, "That seems right to me." After the defense finished, he said, "That seems right to me." Outraged, the concerned parties demanded a decision. "You must do better than that," they protested. "Only a terrible judge would agree with both sides!" Nasrudin replied, "That seems right to me."

I love the stories about Nasrudin, but I hate acting like him. I want ever so much to explain myself, especially to the people I care about most. I want to describe my heart in a way that will make them understand, gain their approval and support, elicit their affirmation. But most will not understand. At worst, they will think I am selfish, lazy, or crazy. At best, if they love me enough, they will accept me without fully understanding me. But can I take the chance? Can I risk the terrible feeling of having the most important thing in my life misunderstood by the people I most love? Often the risk seems too great, and I choose not to take it.

Then I begin to doubt myself. Some people might be able to say, "This is how I feel, and if others don't understand, it is because they are the ones who are blind and deluded." I do not have that degree of confidence, and I am suspicious of it. It comes too close to thinking you have the edge on the truth, a pipeline to God that sets you above other people. That, I know, is not love. But it is yet another reason for self-doubt. If I should speak of my desire, even with fear and humility, people are likely to take me for just that kind of religious fanatic. It is painful not to be understood, but it is real agony to be *mis*understood.

The struggle I am describing is very real. I have made the mistake of trying to speak too much of my heart in places where it was not called for. On such occasions I have been made a fool; I have been left discounted and alone. Once I was trying to encourage a group of pastoral counselors and hospital chaplains to look for God's life of love already happening in their clients. The supervising chaplain said, "Oh, yes. I've heard that before. It's the 'blooming' theory of therapy. Just love the patients, and leave it up to God, and they'll simply bloom into health. Blooming idiocy, I think." I started to say that wasn't exactly what I meant, but I realized it was very close indeed to what I meant, and I didn't know how to go on. I cracked a joke that was uncharitably—albeit deliciously—at the challenger's expense, and changed the subject.

Some years later I was asked by a conference of politicians and church bishops to provide some leadership about decision making. I had just begun to talk about making decisions prayerfully when one of them interrupted. "I don't think we want to hear about prayer right now. We already hear too much from people who know the will of God. I'd rather have some suggestions about how to get them to shut up so we can get on with business." I saw many heads nodding in agreement. I started to defend myself. I said I had virtually no idea what the will of God was in any given situation, and that was precisely why I felt prayerfulness was so important. But even as I was talking, I was aware of how it sounded. They must have been thinking, "If you pray for God's will, but you can't know God's will, then what good is it?" And what could I say? Every honest response I could think of sounded just like old Nasrudin.

Sometimes discretion means it is better not to speak. But it is not so simple as just keeping your heart to yourself. I have learned that in situations like those I have described, the problem was not with my audience but with myself. I was running ahead of grace. When I encountered resistance I not only tried to justify that which cannot be justified; I tried to convince my challengers to agree with me. By that time, my only interests were success and security. My concern was not love, not immediate presence and openness, but to get my point across. I had become a counterfeit evangelist: speaking *about* my heart's desire instead of speaking *from* it.

Real discretion must spring forth from honest consecration. It means taking an immediate prayerful pause and grounding yourself in open, willing hopefulness. If nothing comes out of that God-centered hope, discretion means being silent. If something comes, discretion means taking the risk of acting on it in love, no matter what.[9]

The Fullness of Consecration

So look gently to the source of your motivation, both in speaking with others and in seeking your own truth. Try to let your responses flow out from your heart rather than take the place of your heart. Can you, for a time, just want an in-touch-ness with your deepest longing? Can you just desire desire? If so, and something rises there, own it, cherish it, embrace it. Know it to be your intention and your hope regardless of how you think others might react to it. Turn your heart toward the source, and offer your hope. And in whatever way and to whatever depth is possible, give yourself. Stretch forth and yield. Yield and open.

If you have a community of understanding people with whom you can share some of your experience, so much the better. If not, seek community; pray for it. Even one other person who shares your desire will support you and help you clarify your attempts—and may even help keep you from becoming too bizarre.

Be very honest about what you feel, and pray as directly as you can for the grace and wisdom not to fool yourself. Drop through the superficial turbulence, and seek your deepest desire. Try to get to the bottom, where your feelings no longer have names. There is your most authentic motivation, the source of your most honest intent. And it is love, and always will be.

You may be very clear and specific about your hope, or it may feel vague and general. It may seem very close and powerful, or as far away as a distant dream. You may be able to express it in words or images, or it may be too subtle to even begin to describe. The shape and quality with which you experience consecration may change from day to day; what counts is that you claim what is most real for you now, in this moment.

Sometimes when I pause to sense my desire, it arises in the words "I love you." Most often it seems I am the one speaking; occasionally it seems to be God speaking. There are occasions when the words become "love me," sometimes pleading, sometimes cajoling, sometimes demanding. Again, I am not sure who speaks them, whose desire it is, whether I am the lover or the loved one. Now and then a certain clarity comes in which the distinction between lover and beloved disappears. Then it is only love, expressing itself, enjoying itself, flowing and dancing, or perhaps just being still. At other times, I feel only a yearning, like a hunger, with no words or thoughts. Occasionally it is a sense of gratitude or praise, of peace or comfort, of service or fidelity. Now and then all that is there is a cry for help, for relief, for deliverance.

I have learned from experience that all these things are reflections of the single deepest thing. I shall never be able to capture that deeper truth; all I have is the way it is most authentically manifest in my consciousness in this time and place. It may not feel like enough; sometimes it feels like nothing. But it is sufficient because it is real.

In consecrating your hope, do not be concerned about form or propriety; the sanctity of consecration comes not from structure but from grace empowering your intention to be as involved as you most authentically can be, with God as God is. It is your own unique statement of willingness for something more great, more good, more loving than you could ever dream of, let alone accomplish. It is your best authenticity, your finest sincerity.

Keep risking that your heart's desire is trustworthy. There is always another, deeper step you can take toward more complete trust, a more all-encompassing possibility of love. It will be this way until consecration becomes as ordinary and natural as breathing, until every act of every day is simply sacred, until there is no more separation of life from prayer, until each precious moment, awake and asleep, is consciously, knowingly infused with love, until compassion reigns and justice pervades all things, and until life becomes what it was meant to be: sheer enjoyment and pure dancing in the spaciousness of love.

5

ENTERING THE EMPTINESS

You have made us to be *toward* Yourself, O Lord, and our
hearts are restless until they rest in You.
AUGUSTINE OF HIPPO

Every risk we take for love, each step we take toward greater
consecration, leads us deeper into the spaciousness of love. I have
described many kinds of spaces and emphasized the necessity of
space for consecration; now we must seek a glimpse of the
nature of spaciousness itself. In biblical Hebrew, the letters *yodh*
and *shin* combine to form a root that connotes "space and the
freedom and security which is gained by the removal of constric-
tion." From this *YS* root come words like *yesha* and *yeshuah*,
referring to salvation. When you think about it, it makes sense
that space would be intimately associated with salvation. Space is
freedom: freedom from confinement, from preoccupation, from
oppression, from drivenness, and from all the other interior and
exterior forces that bind and restrict our spirits. We need space in
the first place simply to recognize how compelled and bound we
are. Then we need space to allow the compulsions to ease and
the bonds to loosen. In the Hebrew sense, our passion needs
elbowroom. To the extent that space is permitted by grace and
our own willingness, we discover expanding emptiness in which
consecration can happen, room for love to make its home in us.[1]

It seems to me that spaciousness comes to us in three primary ways. First, it appears as spaciousness of *form:* physical, geographic spaces like the wide openness of fields, water, and sky and the welcoming simplicity of uncluttered rooms. Second, it comes as spaciousness of *time:* pauses in activity when we are freed from tasks, agendas, and other demands. Third, we encounter spaciousness of *soul.* This is inner emptiness, the room inside our hearts, the unfilled quality of our consciousness. Depending upon how we meet this soul-space, we may experience it as open possibility or void nothingness, as creative potential or dulling boredom, as quiet, peaceful serenity or as restless yearning for fulfillment.[2]

The Trouble with Spaciousness

People in our modern developed world are ambivalent about all three kinds of spaciousness. On the one hand, we long for space; in the midst of overactive lives we yearn for peace, stillness, and freedom. We look forward to vacations, and we yearn for our minds to be free of preoccupation. On the other hand, we are liable to become very uncomfortable when such spaces do open up. We do not seem to know what to do with them. We fill up our vacations with activities and compulsions; we fill up our minds with worries and obsessions.

Perhaps I am being romantic, but I think there was a time when we could sit on the front porch and simply enjoy the breeze or watch the sun go down. I remember soft evenings, sitting on my grandmother's lap on the front porch—not a word, barely even a thought. That was simple appreciation. But today many of us have been so conditioned by efficiency that such times feel unproductive, irresponsible, lazy, even selfish. We know we need rest, but we can no longer see the value of rest as an end in itself; it is only worthwhile if it helps us recharge our batteries so we can be even more efficient in the next period of productivity.

Now, on a soft evening, I may retire to my deck (my modern, efficient house does not even have a front porch), and I can just barely recover the old sense of spaciousness and peace I felt with my grandmother. It does not last for long. A few brief blessed moments, and then my mind wants to go back to the work I have yet to do and the worries I feel I must keep picking at. Then I am likely to pour myself a drink. My grandmother never drank; she thought it was a sin. Also, I think, she did not want to fill up her space.

The ancients knew the value of spaciousness for its own sake. The Hebrews ritualized the Sabbath in keeping with God's rest on the seventh day of creation. God did not take that day of rest simply to recoup energy to begin creating another universe during the next workweek. Resting was valuable in its own right. Spaciousness was holy.

The fourth commandment for Jews and Christians is to remember the Sabbath and keep it holy. Many other religions and denominations continue to provide for such times of space and rest, but the meaning has often been twisted. Sabbath was meant to be a day of spaciousness in form, time, and soul. It was to be an uncluttered day, a day not filled up, a day of rest and appreciation, a day of freedom just to be. Now, religious Sabbath is apt to feel like restriction rather than freedom, confinement rather than space. Instead of freedom from having to work, Sabbath came to mean not being *allowed* to work.[3]

I grew up with this kind of reversal. There was a long list of things we were not permitted to do on Sunday. A similar thing was true of silence: silence meant you were not allowed to speak. I shall never forget the liberation I felt when I first went on a silent retreat and the leader said, "The real meaning of silence is that you are free from *having* to speak." Many years later, I came across the following insight from a Tibetan Buddhist text: "Freedom is not the opposite of determinism, but of compulsion, of *having* to act."[4]

We have clearly lost something when we are no longer free just to be, when we must always be active, doing some things and refraining from doing others. Something is missing when we have to force our pauses, carve out our spaces, and then feel we have to justify them. As a result, recreation often means engaging in more pleasurable work, not freedom from having to work at all. The pastor of our church took a sabbatical. He sent regular reports to the congregation about what he was learning. Apparently he felt he had to assure people that he was making good use of his time. Something is amiss when wasting time is something we feel ashamed of, when we must ask a quiet person, "What's wrong?" It is as if a piece of the heart has been cut out; our capacity to be easeful with inactivity has been thrown away and forgotten without our even realizing it.

Think about yourself. How are you when there is nothing to do? When you have a moment of freedom, what do you do with it? Try to take such a moment now: no agenda, nothing to accomplish, just be. Stay with it as long as you can. What happens? Does it feel freeing or confining, peaceful or anxious? Was it different when you were a child? Did it come more easily and feel more comfortable then? If so, what do you think accounts for the change?

Most of us, most of the time, just fill our spaces up or dull our awareness of them. We grab a book, run to the television, work on a project, socialize, have a drink. I used to think women were more comfortable with space than men; nowadays I am not so

sure. Women perhaps feel more guilty about taking time in freedom for themselves, while men feel more anxious. But it is a
tiny difference. Either way, real space can be very unpleasant.

We somehow must realign our attitudes toward spaciousness.
We must begin to see it as presence rather than absence, friend
instead of enemy. This is the most important practical challenge
we face in being consciously in love. It will not be easy, because
we have come to associate space with fear, emptiness with negativity, lack of fulfillment with dysfunction. The seventeenth-century philosopher Benedict de Spinoza said that nature abhors a
vacuum. Modern science has shown he was wrong. There is far
more space than stuff in the universe. The atoms that make up
all matter, including our own bodies, consist of vast distances of
space between tiny subatomic particles. No matter how solid we
may feel, we are much more space than substance. If any nature
abhors a vacuum, it is human nature—and that only because our
nature has been so adulterated by conditioning.

I would ask you again, now, to give yourself a little space.
Take a moment and just sit, just be. Waste some time. See and
hear what there is around you, and notice what happens within
you. Do not expect any particular experience, and do not contrive anything. How does it go?

Space and Repression

It is an addiction of the first order that we feel we must always be
filling up our spaces. It goes along with our addictions to work,
to productivity, to efficiency. Sometimes, though, we do not like
spaciousness because of what appears to us within it. Ever since
Sigmund Freud's work, psychology has understood that human
beings try to keep unpleasant things out of awareness. The psycho-

analysts called it repression or suppression; a more modern term is selective inattention.

At any given moment, we all have a number of worries, fears, guilt feelings, bad memories, and things we are procrastinating about that we are simply putting out of our minds. The difficulty with space, especially interior spaciousness of soul, is that it allows such repressed and suppressed annoyances back into awareness. When I pause for a moment and let my mind settle down, what comes in? The things I have put off, the worries I have been avoiding, the bad feelings I have stifled. Space is like sunlight and fresh air toward which the buried uglies of our souls crawl in search of healing. It is a very healthy thing. Space is not only potentially restful but also therapeutic. But like many therapeutic processes, it can be painful. And in matters of healing consciousness, as in love, there can be no anesthesia.

I know what it is to try to escape from space. A few springtimes ago, I was feeling very overextended and oppressed by my work. I longed for space. A Saturday morning came when there was no one at home and my desk was momentarily clear. Ah, I thought, now I have a chance to just sit, just be for a while. Although I was alone in the house, I closed the doors to my study. I unplugged the telephone, put my cushion on the floor, and lit a candle. I sat down, took a breath, looked out the window, and for the first time in days noticed the beauty of the trees and sky. I closed my eyes and noticed a continuing drivenness deep within me, running on its own momentum. I tried to relax, but couldn't. I prayed. I did some stretching and exercise, and then sat down again. But there was no peacefulness. My mind was yammering—no thoughts, just silly, meaningless noise. I tried to let the tension and the noise be. I prayed some more. This is the way it is, I thought, and I just have to sit through it. My eyes opened, again to seek the sky. I noticed that the doorknob was crooked; I could see from where I sat that the screws had come loose. My toolbox was nearby. When I next thought about seeking space, it was an hour later, and I had the entire door dismantled, off its hinges, screws and knobs all over. That afternoon, when my wife came home and asked me how the day was going, I said, "Great. I fixed the door."

It is also possible to create fake space, in which we force our minds into stillness and keep everything repressed. In fact, it is this fake space that most people associate with meditation and concentration—a forceful, effortful attempt to keep the mind silent, focused, and without "distraction." But this is not space at all. It is instead a kind of trance, a deadening of sensitivity, a stifling and restriction of awareness. It is anesthetized; there is no openness in it, no willingness, no participation. True space is encountered only with the willingness and courage to experience things just as they are.

When people tell me they have trouble taking time for prayer or meditation, I often ask them what unpleasant things they might be wanting to avoid. I often ask myself the same question. My answer right now is ironic; the thing I most want to escape from is my longing for love. It hurts too much, more than anything psychological I have ever experienced. There are many times I would escape it or anesthetize it if I could, but it will not go away. Or perhaps *I* cannot go away.

It is a blessing when love is so relentless, because the more we repress, suppress, procrastinate, or anesthetize, the more resistant we will be toward space. Conversely, the more true space we give ourselves, the less we will repress. And to the extent that we consecrate our spaciousness, intend it for love, point it toward love's source, space will be merciful. The unpleasantness of space will never be more than we can bear. Our increasing availability to the truth happens gradually, gently, with grace. It happens in

keeping with our own unique personalities; we are given what
we need as we need it. Space becomes brutal only if we try to
force it, make it a project, or demand that it meet our expectations.

The Myth of Fulfillment

I have described two basic difficulties we human beings have
with space. In the first, we are addicted to filling up every kind
of space we encounter. We are addicted to fulfillment, to the
eradication of all emptiness. In the second difficulty, we fear
what spaciousness will reveal to us. We would rather have the
anesthetized serenity of dullness than the liberating dis-ease of
truth. Together, our addiction to fulfillment and our flight from
truth weave a harsh, desperate barrier against participation in
love.

Back in the days when I was doing a lot of psychotherapy, a
Roman Catholic priest came to me with this concern: "I'm
nearly fifty years old, and I still don't have my sexuality
resolved."

My response, perhaps a bit too flippant, was, "Join the
crowd."

"No," he said, "I mean it. I'm not satisfied with my relationships, and I can't make peace with celibacy. I can't find any
serenity with my desires for intimacy."

I still felt it sounded quite normal, but he wanted to work on
it. So for several months we explored whether psychological
problems were causing his distress. He had not received perfect
love and support from his parents when he was a child, but I
thought, "Who does?" He had been traumatized in a variety of
ways by early sex education and experiences. I wondered,
"Aren't we all, to some degree?" I couldn't escape my conviction that he was a very normal example of the male of the

human species.

A middle-aged mother told a story not unlike that of the priest. "I should be happy with the way things are. I have a fine marriage, two wonderful kids, a good career. Yet I keep feeling something is missing. I have these dreams about romance. Deep down I am restless; I want something more. I think my sex life is at least as good as the next person's, but there's some kind of intimacy I long for. I think perhaps I am repressing something."

I asked, "Is there any particular reason you feel this is a problem? Could it be that many other people have similar yearnings for something more?" (This was my attempt at a gentler version of "Join the crowd.")

She paused for a long time. "No, I do *not* believe other people have these feelings. I know a lot of people who are perfectly happy and fulfilled."

"Do you think they really are? Or is it maybe just the way they act and talk? I know I hear this kind of thing from many people."

"Well, you talk to a lot of strange people. I have some close friends who never seem to feel the way I do. If they're kidding themselves, they are doing a good job of it. They really feel contented with their lives."

"Have you talked to them? Have you told any of them how you feel, to see what they'd say?"

"No, I haven't. They wouldn't understand. And I'd feel—I do feel—as though there's something wrong with me. They'd give me advice, and that's the last thing I need. I already feel too incapable."

So we explored her psychology for a while. As with the priest, there were imperfections, but again I kept thinking that all experience is imperfect. And I kept wanting to say, "What's wrong with feeling unfulfilled and restless? Isn't there something basically *right* about it?"

With both these people, as with so many others who have confided in me, the real problem was believing that their sense of inner restlessness and lack of fulfillment indicated psychological disorder. They had swallowed the cultural myth that says, "If you are well adjusted, and if you are living your life properly, you will feel fulfilled, satisfied, content, and serene." Stated conversely, the myth says, "If you are not satisfied and fulfilled, there is something wrong with you."

The myth is so widespread that the majority of adults in our culture accept it without question. There are three ways we act out this belief. We may try to "fix" ourselves, our life situations, and our relationships because we feel there is something wrong with them. Or we may repress our restlessness, trying to appear to ourselves and others as if we had achieved perfection. Failing this, we dull our concern altogether, seeking to lose ourselves in work, food, entertainment, drugs, or some other escape. Ironically, all three ways easily become addictions in themselves: addictions to self-improvement, to perfect adjustment, or to various means of escape.

The myth has pervaded virtually every aspect of our society. Popular religion promises peace of mind if only we will believe correctly. If we are not completely happy, it maintains, it is because we are somehow not right with God. Perhaps we are too sinful, or our faith is insufficient, or we have missed the one true doctrine. Countless people believe the religious myth, even when a cursory reading of the lives of saints reveals great agony, doubt, and struggle within themselves and with their world. A slightly deeper probing of spiritual growth shows that as people deepen in their love for God and others, they become ever more open: not only more appreciative of the beauty and joys of life, but also more vulnerable to its pain and brokenness.

Popular psychology promotes the myth as well. It promises

peace of mind for only two categories of people: those who grew up in perfectly functioning families and those who use modern psychology to rise above the scars of their dysfunctional families. Countless people believe this psychological version as well, even when the knotted lives of our most successful citizens are continually displayed in the media for all to examine and when no such thing as a truly functional family can be found.

Although it is very right to treat our real disorders and maximize our health, we make several great mistakes if we think life should or even can be resolved to a point of complete serenity and fulfillment. To believe this is to commit ourselves to a fantasy that does not exist and that, if it were true, would kill our love and end in stagnation, boredom, and death. It is also to remove our concern from the real issues of our life and world, to transfer our energy to a vague, self-serving agenda that must be carried out before we can get on with the business of living, loving, and creating a better world. Further, the myth perpetuates the willful delusion that we human beings are objects, like machines, to be built and repaired, meant for efficiency rather than love. Most importantly, the myth of fulfillment makes us miss the most beautiful aspect of our human souls: our emptiness, our incompleteness, our radical yearning for love. We were never meant to be completely fulfilled; we were meant to taste it, to long for it, and to grow toward it. In this way we participate in love becoming life, life becoming love. To miss our emptiness is, finally, to miss our hope.

The Secret Hope of Emptiness

Emptiness, yearning, incompleteness: these unpleasant words hold a hope for incomprehensible beauty. It is precisely in these seemingly abhorrent qualities of ourselves—qualities that we spend most of our time trying to fix or deny—that the very thing we most long for can be found: hope for the human spirit, freedom for love.

This is a secret known by those who have had the courage to face their own emptiness. The secret of being in love, of falling in love with life as it is meant to be, is to befriend our yearning instead of avoiding it, to live into our longing rather than trying to resolve it, to *enter* the spaciousness of our emptiness instead of trying to fill it up.

It has taken me a long time to learn this secret, and I continue to forget it many times each day. Befriending emptiness is mostly a tender thing, requiring such immediacy and vulnerability that my heart is rendered very delicate. I cannot maintain it, and it is only through the empowerment of grace that it comes to me at all. Yet nowhere else am I more truly myself. In no other way does the woven tapestry of love and addiction spring into vibrant, colorful life.

Some recovering addicts have discovered the secret as they realize that the awesome, terrifying space left by their relinquished addiction is like that of an empty vessel, devoid of substance yet full of possibility. The recovering heroine of Erica Jong's *Any Woman's Blues* finds that "I was not a victim of 'fate.' Yes, God, Goddess, the Higher Power, the Holy Ghost, worked *through* me; I was a human vessel for a divine energy force. But to be a vessel was not the same as to be a victim or a pawn. Life flowed through me, and therefore my body and mind had to be respected."[5]

Some artists have discovered the secret as they endure what Etty Hillesum called the battlefield of our inner space: "To turn one's innermost being into a vast empty plain, so that something of 'God' can enter you, and something of 'Love' too." Etty Hillesum's life came to an end in the concentration camp at Auschwitz, but her hope—and, most amazingly, her joy and gratitude for life—lived on for us through her oppression.[6]

Oppression by other human beings, like the oppression of our own addictions, can teach the secret. But we can learn it only if we have the courage to face our emptiness with undefended clarity. In nineteenth-century Maryland, the young Frederick Douglass was confronted with his own emptiness as he learned to read. "It opened my eyes to the horrible pit, but to no ladder upon which to get out." Douglass was a man of great courage, most obviously in risking his life for freedom for his brothers and sisters. But beneath this, before this, there was a deeper bravery. He was willing to experience the pain of his own longing. He chose not to run away from his truth.[7]

We can perform service to others for a variety of reasons. We can do good deeds because of fear, guilt, or the desire to inflate our egos. But if we really want to be loving, if we truly wish to respond to the call of justice and freedom, we must first have the courage to look into our own emptiness. We must somehow even come to love it. The poet Rilke, a late contemporary of Douglass, advised a young friend to "be patient toward all that is unsolved in your heart and try to love the *questions themselves*. *Live* the questions now. Perhaps over all there is a great motherhood, as common longing."[8]

We all have experiences of emptiness. Some of these experiences, like losing love, youth, or health, or feeling compassion for the pain of others, are universal for the human race. They are expressions of what Rilke called the great motherhood of common longing. But some experiences are always uniquely our own, carried in the secret places of our hearts, touched only in solitude. Anyone who faces emptiness becomes contemplative in that very moment, for then the truth is seen—just as it is.

It is the contemplative saints, however, who most know the fear and pain as well as the joy and freedom of entering emptiness; they have chosen to confront that which has to be thrust upon the rest of us. They have stretched and yielded themselves to experience cleanly and clearly the hunger and brokenness of their own hearts and of our world. They have willingly sought to deprive themselves of anesthesia. They have claimed their desire to bear the beams of love, regardless of the cost.

At the turn of the fifteenth century, Julian of Norwich wrote, "I learned to be afraid of my instability. For I do not know in what way I shall fall. I would have liked to have known that—with due fear, of course. But I got no answer." She faced her fear and was able to continue: "Both when we fall and when we get up again we are kept in the same precious love. The love in which God made us never had beginning. In it we have our beginning."[9]

Spaciousness is always a beginning, a possibility, a potential, a capacity for birth. Space exists not in order to be filled but to create. In space, to the extent we can bear the truth of the way things are, we find the ever-beginning presence of love. Take the time, then; make the space. Seek it wherever you can find it, do it however you can. The manner does not matter, and the experience you have there is of secondary importance. Seek the truth, not what is comfortable. Seek the real, not the easy.

Perhaps you already have an intentional rhythm of prayer, meditation, or reflection. If so, the form may not need to change at all. Just review what you do and what seems to happen. Does your practice allow some real space, or has it become completely filled with spiritual activity? Is it a time of immediate presence for you, in which you can just be? Or has it become a routine in which you find more dullness than wakefulness, more focused attention than openness to what is?

In my experience, all routines sooner or later become habits I begin to hide behind. I can take the best of disciplines—those that are most likely to really enable spacious presence—and turn them into doings. Then I go through the motions of the practice and escape the space altogether. For this reason, I find I need to bring a certain freshness to all my spiritual practices. This time of prayer or meditation may be something I am very used to doing, but why am I doing it now? What is my real hope? Can I reclaim my desire, form my intent afresh, so that I enter each time as if it were the first? Can I claim my hope that it will indeed be a beginning?

If you do not already have such a rhythm, I encourage you to try to establish one. If you are at all like me, this will not be easy. But I am convinced the struggle is worth it; success or failure do not matter—the attempt is worthwhile in and of itself.

The first step is to look for spaces that occur naturally in your life. We all have them, and they can tell us something about what is uniquely right for us. Perhaps you find little natural spaces after you have completed some work, times that you stretch and look around and just be for a moment. Could times like that be expanded? Could you savor them a little longer? Or maybe you sometimes indulge in a long, hot bath, or find yourself in stillness just before you go to sleep or wake up. Possibly you find space in nature or gardening, in music or exercise. Take a while to go over a typical day in your mind—where are the most likely moments of spaciousness? Are there some such moments that you usually immediately fill by watching television, reading, drinking, or some other activity that dulls you even though you call it recreation? Might you be able to just be present a while longer in some of those moments before you move to fill or dull yourself? Might some of them be expanded and made more intentional without causing them to feel too contrived or artificial?

In addition, you should probably at least try to set aside some regular time each day, in the morning or evening or both, that is simply and solely dedicated to just being. In the beginning, these times may be only a few minutes long. (Many of my times are still only a few minutes long, after over twenty years of experience.) A friend of mine began each morning with only the time it took her coffee to percolate. I think there is little value in staying there longer than you can remain fresh and present. When busy-ness and dullness take over, it is probably best to move on and come back again later. On the other hand, don't run away when the first repressed unpleasantness surfaces. Try to let it be; stay a little longer with what is.

A set-aside time in the morning, however brief, can establish a kind of attitudinal posture (*disposition* is the classical word) for beginning the day. It is a time when you can consecrate the day and yourself for the day, offering your prayer for greater presence in love. Likewise, evening times can include a little reflection on the day. Where were the moments of space? What times seemed to contain real presence? What glimpses of being in love were you given? What enterprises or situations kidnapped you and held you hostage to functioning or fear? And where is the spaciousness right now, in this moment at the end of the day? What do you seek there? What is the deepest desire with which you might drift into sleep?

Finally, keep an eye open for longer spaces. Consider extended spiritual retreats, quiet days, or contemplative prayer or meditation groups where you can spend some dedicated and less distracted time just simply being. Bear in mind that I am not speaking of the talk- and activity-filled conferences that are sometimes called retreats or spiritual groups but of periods in which people truly seek stillness and deepening alone or together. Experiment with whether you find space more easily alone or with other people. Look to your own Sabbath—is it possible to claim some time like that for yourself, when just being is truly an end in itself? What sort of support might you need from other people to help you pursue this?

I have proposed that you seek three kinds of spaces in your life: little moments in the midst of work and play, regular set-aside times each day, and periodic longer times of authentic retreat. In all these, and in the rest of your time as well, I hope you will seek the spaciousness of the immediate moment: the spaciousness of *presence.* In this one single moment, here and now, all three kinds of spaciousness come together: form because it is here, time because it is now, and soul because aliveness is birthed in immediacy.

You will, as I do, find yourself resisting the spaciousness of presence. Sometimes you will know that you simply do not want to face into it; it may seem too painful, or it may require too much letting-go of other investments. That is all right. Do not try to force it. If you fight for presence simply because you think you *should,* you will only stifle yourself. True presence never comes through coercion.

But there will be other times, increasingly frequent, when you know that in spite of your resistance you really do desire presence; you want it deeply regardless of the pain it holds or the relinquishment you must endure. When it happens to me, I pray for help: "God, you are here now; help me be here now." Or I repeat one of the precious phrases: "present moment, wonderful moment," "pure and total presence," "practice the presence," "continually renewed immediacy," "be here now," "be still and know," "come unto me," "bear the beams."

I also try to remind myself of what I know from experience: the two most important facts about the spaciousness of the present moment. No matter how full of wonder or how empty and barren the moment seems, *it is always sufficient.* And no matter how much exquisite joy or pain I may feel in the moment, *it will never be more than I can bear.*

The emptiness of the spaciousness of the present moment is sufficient. It contains everything that is needed for lovingly beginning the next moment; it seeks only our own willing, responsive presence, just here, just now. And we can bear whatever experience we have in the spaciousness of this present moment. If we project it into the future it may seem impossible, but just here, just now, it is not too much. There are no exceptions—not in physical pain, not in psychiatric disorder or emotional agony, not in relational strife, not in war, not in oppression, not in loss, not in spiritual aching, not in dying. Love is too much with us for there to be any exceptions.

6

PRACTICE

My heart is ready,
I mean to sing and play for you,
I mean to wake the dawn!
PSALM 57

Authentic spiritual practice is nothing other than consecration in action. It is feeling your deepest desire, claiming it as freshly born hope, offering it to God, and consciously living it as fully as you can. At its best, practice is the active seeking of soul-space and heart-freedom, to ache and to sing, to suffer and to play.

In this sense, practice includes but is not limited to spiritual exercises or methods of prayer and meditation. Practice includes everything you do in life that has a consecrated intent. It is practice to seek a loving, waking presence in your work, to try to be open to that-which-is as you walk or drive or move from place to place, to hope not to forget the divine presence through all your action and stillness.

Practice is participative, prayerful hope, hope to which you are committed, hope for which you have given yourself. You have your own sense of what the hope is for, but it will have something to do with sensing and responding to the gift of love, remembering the divine presence as you move through the activities of your day, realizing—making real—the truth of love's pervasiveness. Practice is the act of living hope—not accomplishment, achievement, or mastery, but active, dynamic willingness. This is the practice of prayerful living, the practice of living love, the practice of the presence of God.

Visions of Practice

The form and atmosphere of practice can be expressed in an endless variety of authentic ways. For example, if you are thinking primarily of God's *transcendence*—God as the holy Other—practice will be like opening your hands to consciously receive, appreciate, and respond to God's gift of love. Or if you are more aware of God's *immanence*—God within you and present in all creation—practice will take some form of being fully and consciously who you are, claiming your desire, expressing your hope and love as completely as you can. If you are especially conscious of your own *will and intention,* practice may be more a matter of psychological acuity: trying to remember, seeking immediate presence, consciously wanting not to be dulled or distracted. If you are primarily aware of being part of the larger *community* of God's people, practice will assume a greater appreciation of humanity now and through history, a willing involvement in shared joy and pain.

Each of these possibilities can be an authentic starting place based on the views and attitudes with which you approach practice. But no particular view is complete in and of itself; the mystery of love keeps stretching our vision. Some people find a more embracing view in the notion of *cocreation.* With this sense, practice is a mysterious interwoven participation of divine grace and human intention. It is God and human beings consciously working, growing, loving, striving, playing, suffering, and celebrating together, but it fits none of our models of togetherness. Cocreation is much more intimate than teamwork, more embracing than fellowship, more expansive than romance, more radical than any structure of human relationship.

Practice can also be seen as a kind of *learning*. Our understanding grows through practice, not so much intellectually, but more in the way we understand rain by walking in it, or learn about the wind by feeling a breeze. The learning that happens through practice is direct, sensate, and hands-on. Practice can lead us to learn many things about ourselves, about other people and the world, about God and love. Some learning takes place gradually, so subtly that we are not even conscious of it. Other learning appears as a breakthrough: a revelation of shining insight. Still other learning occurs with the sometimes painful stripping away of layers of defense and delusion within ourselves, revealing ever more clearly our misjudgments of ourselves, our beauty, our yearning. In this sense, practice is participation in bringing truth to light.

Any participation in love and truth involves us deeply with the world, with other people, with all of creation. Our hearts cannot be open to that-which-is without feeling and responding to the pain, injustice, and brokenness as well as the beauty and hope that exist around us. This response presents us with yet another vision of practice: *intercession*. Intercession means going between or standing in for. Usually we think of intercessory prayer as asking God to help other people, and intercessory action is usually seen as performing a service for those in need. But all consecrated action, all participation in love, has an intercessory quality. A monk in a cloister or a cave—if he or she is truly seeking God—is deeply involved with the needs of the world. The intercessory quality of practice may be subtle, but it is imperative. Without it, something besides love is being sought.

Because of its subtlety, the intercessory dimension of practice is often overlooked. Without our knowing it, consecration can slip into a remote formality behind which we seek self-indulgence instead of real responsiveness to love's call. For this reason, I strongly recommend consciously claiming an intercessory vision of practice along with whatever other views you entertain. In a talk given during one of his visits to Washington, D.C., the Dalai Lama encouraged cultivating "the altruistic mind of enlightenment" by "aiming one's practice at the welfare of others." It can be a simple thing, just turning to God and waiting for someone or something to come to mind, then in silence or words saying, "I dedicate this time for Jane," or "My energies now are for people who are oppressed," or "May the grace that comes through this day bring a little peacefulness to war-torn lands." Let your dedication come from your lovingness, and do not worry it with efficiency questions. I am convinced that our intercessions have a real, practical affect on other people and world situations. I do not understand it, but I do not need to; it is sufficient to remember the power of consecration, the mystery of love, and proceed.

Trust and Risk

No matter how sophisticated our visions of practice may be, there will always be much that transcends our understanding. It is a wonderful friendliness with mystery, a hospitality to unknowing, that allows us to admit at the outset that we do not and need not know exactly what is going on or what lies ahead. At times it may feel adventurous, like traveling uncharted territory. At other times it may seem risky or even dangerous, groping our way in darkness. But there is something trustworthy in consecrated unknowing, because guidance does come through it. It is not the kind of guidance that says, "Do this," or, "Go there." It is instead a direction revealing itself moment by moment in simple, conscious being, in our desire, in our care, in God's graceful participation with our yearning. It is usually not even guidance that we can recognize as such at the time. But in our being as honest as possible and in our refreshing our consecration, it happens. There is a saying sometimes heard in Quaker meetings: "The way opens."

Later, we can look back upon our gropings and recognize how the way did open and recognize the presence of a guiding hand that we did not see at the time. This is true for all of life. You could stop now and reflect upon your own life history. What is responsible for bringing you to where you are today? How much of your life's journey has been the result of your intentional self-determination? How much has been beyond your control? Then, putting it all together, what is it that has seen you through? We are looking at neither determinism nor autonomy here, but a mysterious graceful presence that is deeper than companionship and far more tender than command.

If you feel your life has been rich and rewarding thus far, you are likely to be fairly trusting of the presence of grace. On the other hand, if you see your life as filled with unredeeming trials and pain, your inclination to trust may be impaired by suspicion and defensiveness. But I tell you it does not matter; regardless of how trusting we are, the journey of presence will take us places we would not have chosen for ourselves. Some of these places turn out to be filled with beauty and joy; others show us painful brokenness in ourselves and in our world. At such times what had felt like trust now feels like taking a risk. And it is in the risking, not the trusting, that we most fully live our consecration.

A Basic Practice

Take a little time now, and see if you can put some of these ideas into a concrete experience. No single description of any practice will be just right for you, but the following suggestions will guide you through a primary experience that you can simplify and adapt to your own style and circumstances. If the suggestions seem helpful but you find it awkward to read and follow them at the same time, you might want to speak *your version* of them into a tape recorder and then play it back to yourself.

- Begin by doing what you need in order to "recollect" or center yourself, whatever seems necessary to bring your awareness into the present moment. You may want to take a few deep, relaxing breaths, stretch, and shift your body position until you feel comfortable and awake.

- If you can, offer a little prayer of your honest hope for this time. Do not contrive anything, but see if you can already claim some of your desire.

- See if there is a simple way you can dedicate the time to someone or something beyond yourself. Do persons or situations come to mind as being in special need of grace and healing? If so, offer your practice for their sake.

- Look around; notice the view from where you are. Listen to whatever sounds there are. Especially notice background sounds that you are usually unaware of. Let your eyes and ears be soft and gentle; insofar as possible, just let things be as they are without any extra labeling or judging.

- Notice how your body feels: where there is tension or discomfort, where it feels at ease. Scan softly over your body from head to toe. You need not try to relax, and by all means do not work at relaxing. If relaxation comes naturally, let it happen. If not, let the tension be where it is.

- Be gently aware of your breathing, noticing how your chest and abdomen rise and fall, how the air flows in and out. Try not to change or control it too much. Insofar as is easy, just let it be.

- Now notice what interior sensations and thoughts you have. What is your general mood? What thoughts, memories, images, and feelings are there? Again, do not label or judge these any more than is natural for you; insofar as you can, acknowledge them and let them be.

- Let your attention go deep, gently seeking your most basic desire in this moment. You may need to move through a number of more superficial concerns, thoughts, and feelings, but take your time and seek as much depth as possible. You may not find much of anything, or what you do discover may not be what you expected. It may strike you as pleasant or unpleasant, beautiful or threatening. Sometimes all you can encounter is resistance. Be honest; seek what is real; do not contrive anything.

- Treat what you find with reverence. Acknowledge it even if you find it difficult to bear. If it is honest, then own it as your true stance right now.

- Offer it, offer yourself, to the source of love. Consecrate your hope. Consecrate yourself. I cannot give you specific methods for consecration; we must each find our own way at the time. How it happens will depend on many things: what you have found within yourself, how you feel about it, what God and prayer mean to you, and so on. But do not worry about theological or psychological sophistication—sometimes the most authentic prayerfulness is a simple stumbling stutter, like that of a little child hoping to make his or her desires known. Just let yourself be free, keep it honest, and be as straightforward as possible. If God is God, then God can sort out your mixed feelings, sift through your awkward words, and touch and bless your truth more deeply than you yourself ever could.

- Now, in whatever way you can, open yourself to being in love. Risking and trusting in the goodness and power of love's presence, let your defenses come down, and allow yourself to become increasingly vulnerable. Seek a willingness that is utterly simple and complete, right here, right now, as fully and unreservedly as possible. Do not be concerned about success or failure; do not fight against yourself; do not try to hold on to any particular experience or state of mind. Just seek to be yourself in whatever ups and downs may come, simply wanting to trust in love in each moment.

- If at some point you find yourself trying hard, working at it, adding extra effort, gently notice whether the trying seems natural and in keeping with what you are experiencing, or whether you have slipped into trying to contrive something. If it is the former, let the struggle be. If it is the latter, relax a little, renew your consecration, and come back to the present moment.

- When it is time to move on, refrain from thinking of ending the practice and starting something else. Do not draw a line of separation between this moment and the next. Instead, let your willingness, openness, and trust flow gently into whatever comes next. Your activity and setting may change, but your desire and the interior attitude of your heart can continue for a while. In the way painters "feather out" their brush strokes so there is no distinct line between where one ends and the next begins, feather out your presence.

Simplicity

These steps are designed for set-aside times, when you can take a few minutes for dedicated attention to practice. But the practice is not an end in itself. It is intended as a way of helping you explore and deepen a basic attitude that you can then bring into the rest of your life and activities. At the outset, you may not even be able to get through all the steps in one sitting. Later, with more experience and a lot of grace, all the steps can flow together into one almost instantaneous easefulness, not only in set-aside times but also right in the midst of the most frenzied activity. It really can be that simple.

Please adapt the steps as you need to. For example, if sitting still makes you very tense, you may be able to combine the basic practice with walking, jogging, swimming, or even some simple form of work. Eventually I hope you will be able to bring some aspects of the basic practice into all your activities, all your moments.

Most importantly, subtract anything from the practice that you find unnecessary and overcomplicating. Remember that spontaneous contemplative moments, moments of just being, happen with utter simplicity. Intentional practice should come as close to this naturalness as possible. I would suggest that most of the time, authentic practice does not need to involve doing much of anything beyond being true to your desire. If it is as simple as receiving a gift, then the practice should require no more than an interior, figurative opening of your hands. When you are free to accept such simplicity, it can feel almost sacrilegious to mess it up with extra doings. I know for myself that the more complicated I make things, the more likely I am to be avoiding the truth. There is a maxim from Alcoholics Anonymous: K.I.S.S.—Keep it simple, stupid.

There is also an old Shaker song that says, "'Tis a gift to be simple, 'tis a gift to be free." It is a gift indeed. When we are not free, when we are caught up in too many things, the best thing we can do is pray for the gift of simplicity. Practices can often help us be receptive to the gift, but we need to make sure they are serving simplicity instead of getting in its way. The guiding principle should be to do no more in practice than is needed to help us just be consciously alive in love. When the doings of practice have served their purpose, when they begin to seem like something extra or artificial, it is time to stop doing them.

This is especially important as practice feathers out from set-aside time into normal daily activities. Remember the sacrament of the present moment, the utter here-and-now simplicity in which each precious instant keeps becoming a new precious instant in an ever-fresh cascade of innocent beginnings. Even when it all seems like the same old thing, even when it feels boring and tiresome—and especially when it feels empty—every moment brings forth a hopeful new invitation for greater freedom and deeper love. Never let your ideas of practice interfere with this priceless spontaneity. Instead, allow them to fade into unforced initiative and uncontrived responsiveness. Your consecration continues, more powerfully than ever, but naturalness and easefulness replace artificiality and restraint. Simplicity and freedom arise together, as one thing. The arising movement is often subtle, but it always points toward practice becoming perfectly spontaneous, nothing other than fully and naturally living in love.

Discerning Action

You may wonder how trustworthy your own spontaneity and naturalness are. When a movement toward action arises within you, how do you know whether it is spontaneous naturalness that is grounded in love and truth, or just another conditioned impulsive or compulsive striving? What is the difference between an authentic, abiding desire and a passing whim? Again, your experience will be somewhat different from mine, but let me use mine as an example.

Sometimes when I am trying to be intentional in a practice like the one I have just described, I suddenly feel the urge to shout or to run out of the room and dance down the street. I have felt the same thing sitting in business meetings. Walking through a shopping mall I am occasionally struck with a desire to embrace a complete stranger. I often feel so great a caring and tenderness for the people I work with that I want to grab them and kiss them right square on the mouth. Many times, when I am with people who are very serious and even perhaps in great pain, I suddenly want to laugh.

I want to be spontaneously loving, but I also want to be responsible. I want to do the right thing. I want to be free for the radical movements of love, and I am willing to breach the edges of convention and propriety, but I do not want to do something really wrong or hurtful. How do I know? It would be easy if I could accept a spirituality of continual restraint and passivity; then I could simply try to refrain from acting on any such passion. But it would not be true. Love may be patient, forgiving, and capable of bearing all things, but it does not stifle life.

Many people hold that scripture provides the guidelines for right action, and in a large sense it does. It gives general principles, but scripture is a living, loving word, so it more often deepens my questions about specific situations than gives me answers. Our communities of faith are also there to help us discern what love calls for, but I can't call a clearness committee together every time I am struck by such an urge. Volumes have been written about methods for discernment of spirits in decision making, but in the moment of inspiration there is no time for methods. In the instant, there is nothing other than grace to depend upon, and so I pray. It is fast, almost instantaneous prayer for guidance. God, however, does not usually come through with instructions. When I want a specific answer for a hard question, I most often hear-feel a sense of "trust in me" or some similarly beautiful but unhelpful thing. Now and then I will get right down to it in a spoken dialogue with God. I ask questions, and answers come. Then, of course, I wonder if it is God or my own ego. So I ask God, "God, is that You or me?" The response comes back, "Yes."

Oh, well. Nowhere in any scripture does it say that God will not be frustrating. If God does not come through with specific directions and explanations for me, I can hardly tell you how to discern between radical loving and impulsive grasping, between spontaneous naturalness and passing whim. I am often very angry with God for hiding from me when I feel so alone and for refusing to give me instructions when I want to do the right thing. But most of the time, when I have my wits about me, I am truly grateful. There is no other way that God can honor my freedom; I know that the divine One hides lovingly.

Left with an unknowing dependence on grace in the instant of an arising desire, we very often truly do not know what to do. As frustrating and painful as the dilemma may be, there is a real beauty in it. It is precisely at those times of not knowing that we are most alive in realizing our need for grace. If you really think about it, I believe you will see that your love is greater, more full and awake, even, perhaps, more joyous at such times than at any time of certainty. Abundance of life comes most clearly when God does *not* provide the answers. It does not keep me from wanting the answers or even from raving and despairing in their absence, and it does not give me much peace of mind in the immediate situation, but truth be told, I would have it no other way.

Unknowing means having to trust in God's presence, love, and goodness. It does not mean we are completely on our own, nor does it mean we are without resources. In a strange mixture of abandonment and affirmation, unknowing may reveal that we actually appreciate more of the truth than we realize.

I am sure you already have within yourself a sense of what it feels like when you are driven by compulsion, grasping, and fear. You know from your own experience what it is to rush ahead of grace, to try to take things into your own hands and make them come out the way you want. You know what it is to feel you are on your own, with nothing and no one to trust beyond your own frantic strategies.

You also know something of what it is like at the other end of the scale, where you feel powerless and victimized. You have a sense of the degradation that comes with being a pawn or a puppet, determined neither by love nor will but by the expectations of other people, by the rules of propriety, by your own addictions, or by the winds of circumstance.

Think about it. Recall situations in which you have touched the extremes of the spectrum between lonely autonomy and demeaning passivity. At one end there seems to be nothing but your own willpower to see you through. At the other it is as if your will does not even exist. If you can recall—or even imagine—what it feels like at these extremes, you have a good and quite substantial guideline for making on-the-spot decisions: *If it feels like that, don't do it.*

You have access, then, to a caution, a "don't do it." Is there a positive guideline to complement this negative one? Is there a "do it"? Psychologically, we might try to find the middle of the spectrum and live there. Indeed, that is the place of psychosocial health and efficiency. It has been called self-affirmation, assertiveness, emotional maturity, individuation. You know something about what this feels like as well. There have been times when you had a reasonably good sense of yourself, a certain quality of integration and well-being. It is a nice way to feel.

And indeed you can recall the feelings associated with the middle ground and compare them to your sense of any present choice. This is a good common-sense guideline, but I cannot go so far as to say that if it feels like that, do it.

The problem is, God does not take up residence on this or any other spectrum. Love finds no steady home in psychological health. I am sure God wants us to be whole and healthy in every way possible, but love neither depends upon these things nor ends with them. In fact, blessings sometimes come through brokenness that could never come in any other way. In reflecting on my own life, I have to conclude that grace has come through me more powerfully sometimes when I have been very dysfunctional and maladjusted. Love transcends all possible adjustments and continually invites us through and beyond them. God invites us to a communion of divine and human desire that cannot be located in any concept or model. We must go beyond the spectrum entirely.

This does not mean we must become very mystical or otherworldly. The evidence of our experience of being in love is just as solid as anything else; we simply have to look for it consciously. I have already asked you to look for your own evidence several times; I have encouraged you to recall moments of just being in love, contemplative moments, times of authentic presence. I would ask you to do it again now, but add the language of discernment. What are some occasions on which you have felt closest to divine presence, most fully, freely, lovingly present yourself? You may feel you have never fully experienced it, but what is the closest you have come? Recall what it felt like, and that, with prayer, is your guideline. If it does feel like that, and you have grounded yourself in prayer, do it.

It was Saint Augustine who said we could love God and do as we will. Many would say this is too simplistic or downright dangerous, but I encourage you to consider it prayerfully. As I have said before, you can choose primarily to love God or fear evil, to seek heaven or fear hell. If you choose the side of fear, you are likely to stifle your love by trying to make sure you never make a mistake. If you choose love, you will surely make some mistakes, but you will be growing and making a difference in the world around you. I hope you will feel free to disagree with me here, but on balance, I would prefer a thousand mistakes in extravagance of love to any paralysis in wariness of fear. Our world has known too much of fear, defensiveness, and mistrust; I think we could use a healthy dose of unmitigated, mistake-making loving.

If you must have a qualification, as I usually do, ask yourself and God whether your choice might really hurt someone. If you sense that it could, proceed with care. Make use of all the resources available to you. But do proceed; do not let fear control you. Have you ever wondered why, when the people of both Old and New Testament stories are confronted directly by divine presence, someone has to come along and say, "Be not afraid"? In the same way that prayer is precarious, acting in love is a fearful thing, and it demands of us the greatest trust in God—which is our only true courage.

Stretching and Yielding

Sometimes, whether we choose it or not, fear does control us. Then, though we still desire to choose a more loving way, we find ourselves so caught up in worries and preoccupations, so tense and hard that it is just impossible to have any real sense of open, natural, prayerful presence. At such times we are likely to want to try harder, to make it work the way we want. A touch of this is good—it expresses our dedication in a forthright way. But most of us are likely to overdo the trying. We forget our dependence upon grace and turn our prayerful practice into a

self-propelled project. Then consecration becomes concentration, dedication becomes determination, fidelity becomes stub-
bornness, willingness becomes willfulness.

I have found the concept of stretching and yielding to be a
wonderful alternative to willfulness. We can stretch toward
something without having to grasp it, stretch ourselves open to
receive something without having to hold it. Physical stretching
helps us participate in our bodies instead of seeing them as
objects. We can stretch our minds without feeling we must comprehend everything. We are stretched by the circumstances in
which we find ourselves, and we can choose to stretch ourselves
in meeting them. We can stretch our wills forward in intention,
stretch open our hearts in consecration.

But stretching alone is pointless; it always must be followed by
yielding. Physical stretching is an active tensing of muscles and
ligaments in preparation for yielding. The yielding may be active,
allowing some muscles to relax while others contract, some joints
to flex while others extend in order that movement can be flowing and effective. Or the yielding may be passive, allowing all the
muscles to become increasingly relaxed. Biologically, stretching
and yielding make the natural transitions between action and rest,
rest and action. Watch a cat stretch and yield before it lies down
or as it gets up. Cats know how to do it.

Notice also how infants stretch and yield, how relaxed they
are when asleep, how vital when awake. The reason is, they are
not working against themselves. Natural stretching and yielding
flow in harmony. We have all marveled at how a baby's grasp on
a finger can be so powerful, how such tiny muscles can be so
strong. The physical answer is simple. In grasping, the flexor
muscles on the palm side of the hand and arm must contract
while the extensor muscles on the other side relax. A baby does
this almost perfectly. Most adults contract muscles on both
sides—it goes along with "trying hard"—so the flexor muscles

have to work harder to close the fingers. We work against our-selves. We get stuck in our stretching.

Do not equate stretching and yielding with activity and rest. Activity and rest are states of being for muscles, organs, minds, wills, hearts. Stretching and yielding are transitions between these states of being, which—if allowed to happen naturally—permit a continual flexibility and flow instead of one frozen con-dition. Translated into the wholeness of our being, stretching and yielding are the way of joining in the ever-evolving rhythms of love. Stretching and yielding, we enter reunion and repose, activity and creation.

More than three thousand years ago, in the Chinese philoso-phy that eventually became Taoism and Confucianism, the strong, firm, stretching-forward force of *ch'ien* and the receptive, yielding force of *k'un* were considered the father and mother of all universal processes. Together, they formed t'ai chi, or "ridge-pole," the primal beginning of all things. In later Chinese thought, they became the well-known yang and yin of universal harmony.[1]

When stretching and yielding flow together in harmony, will-ingness is freed, consecration is empowered, love unfettered, fear conquered. The harmony cannot be achieved through willful strategies; it must be *allowed* to emerge as we are given the grace to simplify our presence and cease unnecessary complications. Go back to the basic practice for an example. If tension makes it difficult to settle into the practice, take some time to see if you can stretch the tense areas of your body and allow them to yield into more complete naturalness.

Stand up and stretch your body. Stretch and shake out your arms and legs like an athlete warming up. Lean forward and back to stretch your trunk—only so far as is comfortable. Roll your head in a small circle to stretch your neck. Clench and relax your hands; curl your toes up, then spread them; point your toes down, then up. Shift your position until you find some comfort, and let yielding happen naturally as you move through the first steps in the practice.

If tension and agitation are still getting in your way when it comes time to be aware of your breathing, you can also do some stretching of your breath. Take control of your breathing and make it work for a while, then let it go; yield it to naturalness. A deep sigh is one kind of natural breath-stretch; yawning is another. Try a sigh or two; encourage a yawn.

The same thing can happen as you sift through your feelings toward your more basic desire. If you find this difficult, stretch your mind and attention by concentrating on one thing for a while. Work at it, as if you were stretching the concentration muscles of your mind. Then, as with muscles and breathing, let it go. Let your attention be free; yield it and see what happens.

As you move through your day, keep a gentle eye open for times of natural stretching and yielding, and try to let it happen fully. You will notice your body wanting to stretch more frequently. If you feel a yawn coming, do your tactful best not to stifle it. Explore the possibilities of natural stretching and yielding in thought, feeling, relationships, sensation, work, and play. How do these affect your presence, your consecration? How does consecration affect stretching and yielding? What is your sense of grace through it all?

A Syllabus of Practice

Thus far I have woven specific suggestions for practice into a wide-ranging discussion. The following chapters will examine specific forms of practice. As a transitional summary, I offer the following list of suggestions. As you review the list, prayerfully keep your eyes open for what seems to be harmonious with your own natural seeking of love. Use my words to help you affirm and nurture what is already happening within you. Where my words differ from your experience, let them challenge you but do not feel compelled to follow something that feels artificial. The source of love has been encouraging, protecting, and inviting you all along; your true guidance will continue to come from that source, not from anyone else's words.

- Prayer: Surround your practice with prayer, prayer at the beginning, prayer through the middle, prayer at the end—which is the next beginning. Pray impulsively or reflectively, in a flash or with great care, in silence or aloud, in inexpressible desire or poetic beauty, in helpless, stuttering dependence or demanding desperation; pray in whatever way you can, but pray. Be as honest and straightforward as possible, and keep reminding yourself that you are not alone in your desire. From before all time, it has been and will be more God's desire than yours, and the invitation is not to take it upon yourself in some controlling way but to participate with all your being.

- Space: Set aside at least one time each day for real, dedicated prayerful presence. Morning times help you consecrate the day. Evening times offer prayerful reflection on the day and consecration of sleep. Savor shorter times in the midst of your daily activities as opportunities to come home to your heart and renew your consecration. As frequently as possible, take one or more whole days of retreat. Seek real Sabbath, in which you can more deeply let yourself be you and God be God.

- Immediacy: Remember the sacrament of the present moment. Yield into the here and now as fully and frequently as possible. This does not mean to refrain from thinking about the future or the past; it is simply realizing the present no matter what is going on. Cultivate hope instead of expectation, and each instant will become the next in graceful ease.

- Transition: Let all your changes be soft. Feather the transitions between quiet times and activity, between aloneness and relationship, between wakefulness and sleep, between one situation and the next. If you say "amen" after a prayer, do not let it mean "the end." Recover its original meaning of acknowledgment: "So be it," "Indeed," or simply, "Yes."

- Community: Remember that just as you cannot deepen love without the grace of God's transcendence intervening in your life, you also cannot do it without the grace of God's immanence arising in human relationships. You need the support and challenge of spiritual friends. Be open to finding such people. They are around, they come as gifts, and sooner or later grace will bring you together. No matter how painful it may be, keep searching for a deeper grounding in your tradition of faith, in scripture, and in communal worship.

- Intercession: No matter how alone you may feel, you are irrevocably involved with everyone and everything. If you are not involved by seeking love and light, you are involved through your fear and darkness. Acknowledge this, and participate consciously by dedication of your practice for the welfare of others.

- Desire: You may ache for the direct experience of God's presence, for absolute intimacy with other people and the rest of creation, for wholehearted living in love. Or you may be in touch with only the slightest hint of wanting. Be it strong or weak, never relinquish your yearning, but judge yourself by neither its satisfaction or its frustration. Whether or not you feel the presence of God, it is your wakeful presence, your consecrated and hungry participation, that counts.

- Presence: Your willing presence in the world is absolutely precious and deeply needed. Therefore never think that you must escape from the world in order to be centered and recollected. Instead, find your spaces within the real stuff of life and within the real stuff of yourself. Retreat and Sabbath space are natural parts of the real world, not islands apart from it. Quiet and stillness serve our deeper entry into that which is, not withdrawal from it. See and hear and feel what is around and within you. Acknowledge it, and respond as love invites you to.

- Consecration: Your hope, birthed from your claimed desire, is a baby you embrace and offer for God's blessing. When you consecrate your hope, you also consecrate yourself: your willingness for love and your dedication to life. Do not be concerned about the form your consecration takes. We will all be stumbling and faltering in such holiness. Just be sincere. As we are with our own children, the source of love cannot help but be touched by our awkward sincerity.

- Simplicity: In responding to that which is, seek the simple, natural processes of stretching and yielding. Simplicity is gained neither by force nor by indulgence. Simplicity already exists beneath all our complications and is increasingly revealed as the complications relax. In practice, do no more than necessary, and when it is no longer necessary, stop.

- Trust and risk: Trust in love where you can, and where you cannot trust, risk. There is something that has seen you through thus far, and its goodness is worth risking. In risking, trust grows. In trusting, faith is given. In faith, all things are possible—more than we could ever hope or imagine.

- Play: Love is the serious work of the universe, and at the same time it is absolute play. In fullness of love, the exuberance of life expresses itself freely. Remember the wisdom that says freedom is liberation from compulsion. As freedom grows, work and play blend, laughter erupts, love dances.

- Discernment: Pray always. Claim your experience and your God-given wisdom in considering how to act. But most of all, let yourself fall in love; let yourself be loved and be in love in whatever surprising ways you may encounter. Seek light more than you fear darkness. You need not throw caution to the wind, but do not let fear control you. Fear hurts, and it can sometimes be worthwhile in getting your attention, but as a way of life, fear is never worth it. Love hurts too, but it is always, ever, worth it.

With these principles as a background, we will now explore some specific practices that can apply to every moment of every day. The next four chapters address four ways of practicing loving presence that Brother Lawrence identified three hundred years ago. Brother Lawrence did not invent them; he only brought to them his unique simplicity and humble style. The ways themselves have existed for millennia. They are not in the least dusty with age. Like the present moment they seek, they are ever fresh and always new.

7

THE LITTLE INTERIOR GLANCE

Having found different methods and practices to attain
the spiritual life in several books, I decided that they would
serve more to hinder than to facilitate me in what I
was seeking.
BROTHER LAWRENCE

Brother Lawrence had more than his own sense of humor; he touched the laughter of God. There is much in love that is terribly painful, but even a taste of the exuberance of God's love brings irrepressible joy. The lightest and most ordinary encounter with the laughing God happens in the little instant of remembering love after we have been forgetful. For me it is one of the most precious experiences of living: to have been kidnapped by some worry or striving and then suddenly to be gracefully returned home to the present moment and reminded of love. It is almost always an occasion for giggles.

Scores of such little homecomings happen every day, and I cherish them more than diamonds. It is because of these moments of remembrance—which can happen only after my attention has been pulled away somewhere "else" by my attachments—that I am profoundly grateful to be addicted. Of course I seek greater freedom for love and understand the tragedy of major addiction, but I honestly do not wish for complete liberation in this life. If the one great homecoming were to happen too soon, I would so miss all the many little ones.

It is said of Brother Lawrence that when something had taken his mind away from love's presence he would receive "a reminder from God" that so moved his soul that he "cried out, singing and dancing violently like a madman." You will note that the reminders came from God and were not his own doing. But Brother Lawrence did suggest many things to do. In spite of his difficulties with methods and practices, he knew that dedicated practice is a necessary expression of consecration.[1]

The first of Brother Lawrence's ways is precisely the little homecoming of which we have been speaking: the reminding, the remembering, the wonderful returning to love's present moment. He called it the little interior glance. The interior glance does not necessarily mean looking inward; it simply *happens* interiorly. It is a contemplative look Godward. It is an attitude of the heart leaning toward the truth of God's presence, or a flash of the mind opening to the remembrance of being in love. It might involve a thought about God here and there during the day, feeling our desire for love now and then, performing small consecrated actions, leaving little reminders for ourselves, or anything else that can help pull us out of our forgetfulness for a moment. Little interior glances are simple things: unadorned remembrances and noticings happening within the ordinary activities of our daily lives. They come and go. They are not to be held on to.

Encouragement

Little interior glances are rooted in our deep, abiding desire for love and God's desire for us. We often forget the deep, enduring constancy of love, but the glances spring forth to remind us.

They are like iceberg tips, flashing for a moment when sunlight breaks through the clouds of our preoccupation. We can encourage the glances by both intending them and praying for them.

The most profound encouragement comes, I think, by just being yourself in the present moment. But it is also helpful—within that present moment—to look to the future and remember the past. If you have a little quiet space in the morning, you can acknowledge your desire for love and reclaim your hope to remember love's presence during the hours to come. You can briefly scan through the activities planned for the day and perhaps identify times when you will likely be most forgetful. You might think of something to help you remember especially during those periods. Most important, you can pray for the grace of homecomings in the day ahead. Ask God, directly and without qualm, to shower you with glances. Ask God to remind you of God.

If you can also take some space later in the day, you will find it very helpful to review the preceding hours and reflect on how your presence has been going. If you only have one set-aside time each day, you can still think back over the past twenty-four hours before looking to the future. The reflection can take many forms: journaling, writing poetry, drawing or painting, or just sitting prayerfully. Feel free to experiment, but try to keep it simple. Don't make a big deal of it, but consider asking yourself some questions that cover the following territory:

- At what times during the past day did I seem to be most present, most immediate, most consciously available in love?

- When did I seem most absent, most kidnapped or closed off?

- What seemed to help or hinder my presence?

- How do I feel right now about how it has been going? Am I grateful, frustrated, joyful, angry, exuberant, bored, at peace, afraid? Can I honestly present my feelings to God right now, just as they are?

- Are there any changes I want to make, any special help I seem to need, any prayer that expresses my present hope and intention for the time to come?

The words I have used here convey the general idea, but they are not your words. Rephrase the questions to fit your own language and experience. I hope you will take time to do that and to keep revising and simplifying them as your experience changes and deepens. Later on—and perhaps you sense it even now—I suspect the questions will coalesce and explode into the one great question: Am I truly becoming more loving?

Willful Resolutions

Be gentle with your intention as you go through the kind of reflections I have suggested. As you remember the day just past or think about the day ahead, you will be tempted to make resolutions like "I am going to try hard to remember." Don't do it, and if you catch yourself doing it, stop. Resolutions mean willpower, willpower means achievement, achievement means success and failure, and the whole sequence means losing an appreciation of the gift. I have learned two sure things in the struggle between my desire for love and the oppression of my attachments. The first is that God is absolutely trustworthy. The second is that resolutions are absolutely not.

You will also be tempted to try to hold on to a sense of presence, to make a steady state of it. It will not work. If you are lucky, you'll just miss the moment and be frustrated. If you are successful in holding on, things will be much worse. At some point you will discover that what you are holding is not real; it is something you yourself have contrived. You will also discover that you have been suppressing and deceiving yourself in order to keep it.

During a recent retreat, a friend of mine had to leave to attend a business meeting. He tried to maintain the sense of presence he had had at the retreat throughout the meeting. He thought he had been able to do it, and was quite grateful until a few hours later when he was beset with feelings of rage, abandonment, and fear. In trying to hold on, he had forged a falsehood and not allowed his natural responsiveness to emerge. When he finally relaxed his repressive charade, a deluge of negativity engulfed him.

In making resolutions and in trying to maintain a state, we are naturally expressing our deep desire for wakeful presence in love. But it is a wrong way of expressing it. This way becomes willful so quickly and insidiously that we lose touch with our relationship with grace. It is by no means the end of the world if we find ourselves in such a predicament; I know it well, because for at least a decade I spent most of my days there. God did not forget me while I was trying so desperately to create my own experience of God. And grace, thank God, is not dependent upon our state of mind.

Some traditions would disagree with my advice. Much of the spirituality of the early Christian desert, for example, advised using all one's mental strength to hold on to remembrance of Christ. Some Hindu and Buddhist disciplines encourage a similar forcefulness. Such effortful concentration may have a place in monastic settings and can be helpful as a temporary mental stretch before yielding into simple presence. But I do not recommend it as a steady diet for people who live in the world of families, homes, and workplaces. I have tried it myself, and it only created great trouble for me. I became depressed and irritable inside and absolutely obnoxious around friends and family.

Resolutions and grasping are not good ways to go about receiving a gift. There is a vast, spacious difference between consecrated hope and willful expectation. I suggest you become familiar with the feeling you have inside when you make a resolution or strive to cling to something. You can call the feeling up inside you right now: the tight sense of grasping, the "I have to" attitude that borders on guilt or desperation, the tense and forceful atmosphere of need. Get to know the feeling well, so that whenever you feel it you can stop what you're doing, take a breath, relax, yield a little, and let your real self turn to the real God. Substitute prayer for resolution, hope for expectation, fidelity for compulsion. Seek to encourage yourself instead of manipulating yourself. Cultivate your receptivity to the little interior glances instead of grasping for them. Live, love, and yearn with unbearable passion, but don't try to make it happen and don't try to hold on when it does happen.

Absence Becoming Presence

After any time of appreciating love's presence, "feather yourself out." Yield yourself into the next moment, the next situation, the next thing you need to do. The next moment may be very fresh and different, but it is still the present moment; the present is never ending and always beginning. If you gently cultivate an appreciation of love rather than try to maintain it, your presence can continue from one moment through the next for a surprisingly long time.

But it will go away; it is bound to. You must be free to let it come and go. If you have to move from quiet into a noisy household or a busy office, for example, your immediate presence will probably be gone before you know it. When you notice its absence there is no need for self-criticism or heroic endeavors to recapture it. Remember that it was a gift in the first place, that whatever you might be able to recapture would not be the real thing, and that what you are thinking of is already in the past. Right here, right now, there is a fresh, new moment. Come here, into now. *This* is your little interior glance.

Do try to savor little spaces whenever you can throughout the day. No matter how busy you are, there are always moments between activities when you can take a breath or two and intentionally glance Godward. If you have a regular schedule, you can plan some moments ahead of time. You might take a few minutes after the kids get off to school, or when the youngest goes down for a nap, or between your coffee break and your next meeting, or before or after lunch.

The length or form of these times is not as important as how often you can find them. How often you find them is not as important as finding them at least now and then. And even finding them now and then is not as important as wanting them. Pray for them. And, as best you can, remember how much you want them.

I assure you that as grace increasingly empowers your consecration, your absences will become less frequent and less prolonged—and when you do go away, you won't go very far. The most wonderful thing, though, is that each recognition of having been away becomes an instantaneous homecoming. It is a blessing given in a microsecond, a little interior glance just happening without your needing to do anything at all. It will probably come with a giggle. And it will be sufficient.

Brother Lawrence came to a point where the little glances were given with each instant. They sprinkled upon him so lavishly that his whole life became remembrance, his immediacy continually renewed. What happened to him can happen to anyone. You don't need to be in a monastery; it can happen anywhere. When you are caught up in the very real demands of your family and friends and work, a monastery might look attractive. A cave might seem even more desirable. It might even feel wonderful, for a few days. But then there you would be, still carrying all your addictions and resistances, and the present moment is beginning again.

If you think monasteries make it easy, talk to the monks. It is not easy anywhere. But it really can happen. Regardless of who or where you are, the little glances are given. With consecrated hope, the whole race of humanity can be made delicate by grace. I am certain God nearly dies in each instant from the unbearable yearning to have it be so, and the agony of how far away we are. I am certain also that it *is* happening. And I have no doubt that God is rendered inexpressibly happy in each instant, so tenderly pleased, when one single human heart, in the tiniest little glance, knows its own longing for love, because that longing is God's own. In this very instant, in this immediate now, thousands of human hearts are glancing Godward. It is happening, and it is the hope of the world.

Forgetting

If we want something badly enough, you would think we would remember it. It is very easy to remember our desire for food when we are hungry. And we certainly do not forget to satisfy our addictions. But our hunger for love is different. We have very little freedom to deny either our physical needs or our addictions. Such cravings are harsh with us; they drive us, compel us, obsess us. We cannot "just say no" to them.

But we have immense freedom with our desire for love. Real love can never be coercive; God relentlessly keeps us free even when we wish it were otherwise. If we were not able to say no to love's invitation, we would not be able to authentically say yes. If we could not easily forget God, our remembrance would not be fully loving, and the little glances would lose their sparkle. To put it another way, God refuses to become an object of addiction. We develop all kinds of addictions to images of God, systems of belief, and particular expressions of love, but we can never be addicted to the true God or to God's true love.[2]

I have spoken of the Divine One hiding lovingly from us. A pastoral counselor friend explained it as God's game of hide-and-seek. The game is not completely fair. When God hides from us, we can find the hiding place only when and if God chooses. But when it is our turn to hide, God always knows right where we are. The game is not always fun; sometimes it feels like abandonment. But when the seeker finds the hider, it does not matter who has won; both are overjoyed. The source of love has the advantage all along, but it is our advantage as well. God spoke a promise through Jeremiah: "When you seek me you shall find me—when you seek me with all your heart, I shall let you find me."[3]

God has an infinity of hiding places. We may discover God anywhere: in people, in nature, sometimes most surprisingly in ourselves. But we have only one hiding place, and there we can hide only from ourselves. Because we live and move and have our being in God, we can hide only in our forgetfulness. We may complain that God is hidden, but we hide incessantly. In one moment we fervently claim our desire for love as the most important thing in life. In the next instant we have forgotten; something else has become all-important to us.

It is because of our hiding in forgetfulness that the little interior glances are so precious. Each glance is a remembrance, an emergence from forgetfulness. Whether we find God directly with our glance is not so important; we have found ourselves in love. Each noticing points us homeward, and God who is our true home knows right where we are.

Remembering

The practicalities of remembering are a good example of stretching and yielding. Because there are many forces in and around us all that force us into forgetting, your first and foremost act must be stretching toward God for the grace of remembering, asking God to remind you of God. Then yield into a hopeful receptivity, a conscious desire to be surprised by glances given to you through the day.

In addition—or better, as an outgrowth of your prayer—you can do a wide variety of things to encourage yourself to remember. The formal and informal spaces you can find will help a lot. So does gathering with those few people in your life who truly appreciate and support your desire: your real spiritual community. It is a powerful reminder simply to be in the presence of such friends. Just a phone call, a postcard, or even a passing thought of your friends can do the same thing. Similarly, look at your formal religious participation. Worship services are in part intended to help you remember what is most important in your life. Do they do that for you? Are there ways you can help make them better reminders?

You can also sprinkle your experience with physical reminders. When you have something important to remember, how do you normally try to keep it in mind? Do you make notes to yourself, tie a string around your finger, or ask someone else to help remind you? Whatever has helped you remember other things can also help remind you of God's presence, and you should use as many of these methods as possible. At first it may seem a little silly to tie a string around your finger to help you remember your desire to be in love, but if it works, why not? What kinds of reminders have worked for you in the past? What new things might hold promise?

If tying a string around your finger seems just too absurd, think of it as the hide-and-seek game. Or consider that this entire enterprise has contained a certain silliness from the beginning. What could be more goofy than passionately yearning for what has already been given, devotedly seeking the love in which we are already immersed? So you might as well get out of your efficiency mind and let the chips of your self-image fall where they may. There is no advantage in waiting to acknowledge your foolishness. Better to admit it now, take a bit of pride in it, and get on with it. There is no time to waste on practical things.[4]

Try switching your watch to your other wrist, or your ring to another finger, remembering when you notice the feeling of difference. Some people set their digital watches to beep on the hour as a reminder. Leave little notes or symbols where you will encounter them: in your calendar or on your mirror, on your desk, behind the milk in the refrigerator, on the steering wheel of your car. These might be real memos like "Remember," or little pieces of scripture or poetry. Maybe a small leaf or twig, or a pebble here and there might be better than written notes. Do you remember the line "Put a pebble in my shoe"? It works.

You might experiment with wearing some dedicated, symbolic article of clothing or jewelry. Consider wearing a symbol of your faith. Think about wearing it beneath your clothing, where you can feel it against your skin. If you wear it where others can see it, then think about your motivations. Whom are you wanting to remind? If you wear a public symbol, consider making it big enough so that people will think you are a religious fanatic. Then their raised eyebrows can be your reminder.

Other people can be the best reminders of all. Look for the divine presence in other people's eyes, or let the faces of people on the street be little homecomings into precious immediacy. Don't turn your eyes away from people you meet. Spend an extra moment looking at a sleeping child.

You can tag places, objects, and sounds with reminding significance. If there are special things in your house or office or special places that you pass while driving your car, you can dedicate them. "I hope to remember love's presence every time I pass this table (or picture, or plant) or whenever I hear birds singing (or children laughing, or doors slamming)." When I drive from my home to the Shalem Institute office, part of the trip is through beautiful Rock Creek Park in the District of Columbia. Years ago I dedicated that stretch of road to remembrance of God. Sometimes I forget and just drive on through, but more often the dedication comes back to me, and there I am. From the office we can hear the bells of the National Cathedral. Often I am so absorbed in some other foolishness that I don't even notice them. But when I am the least bit present, they offer me the little interior glance. It is, of course, what they were meant to do.

If you work in an office, you could dedicate your paper clips, or the bell on your typewriter. If you know what you are doing, you can program your computer to read out a prayer every so often. The Shalem mailing list runs on a program that says prayers for everyone. If your trip between home and office is not as beautiful as mine, you could dedicate a nondescript shopping center, a billboard, or some unknown family's house. At least twice a day, there it is.

Also consider dedicating repeated activities. In the same way that noticing your breathing can bring you home, any other physical activity can serve the same purpose: walking, laughing, sitting, lying down, yawning, making dinner, taking a shower, mowing the lawn, feeding the kids, installing a particular part in an assembly line, using a certain tool on a construction site—anything.

Look at the things you do regularly in your work, travel, and recreation. Some of these are natural, built-in reminders that you can cultivate. Other activities seem to automatically seduce you into forgetfulness; these might be worth giving a little special attention. For example, I spend a lot of my time writing, and writing is a natural reminder for me. I feel very dependent upon God as I write; it is an inherently prayerful activity. By contrast, building a bookcase in my workshop, writing computer programs, and tuning up my car's engine are occasions for forgetfulness. These activities capture me the same way fishing does; they pull me into a trance. I try, very gently, to plant some reminders in such activities. I notice the feel and smell of the wood, I program prayers into the computer, I invite God's presence into my consciousness as I work on the car. (Fishing, for me, is hopeless.) Look at where you are most likely to remember and to forget; are there some small prayers you can offer and some little things you can do to enhance remembrance and ease forgetfulness?

The Emptiness of Desire

Try a little gentle asceticism, a little doing without. The classical spiritual practice is fasting. Fasting has many meanings and effects, but to notice a little physical hunger now and then can be a beautiful reminder of the deeper hunger of our souls. Fasting generally applies to eating, but you can fast from any habitual activity: watch a little less television; smoke a little less; refrain just a bit from expressing your opinion; hold back a little from being competitive; don't spend quite so much time worrying about things; don't be quite so stingy or judgmental; extend yourself when you are caught up in self-indulgence; indulge yourself when you are doing everything for others.

What works as fasting for you will depend on the specific activities to which you are addicted. The only important factor is that you have made a habit of it, so when you curtail it you will be left with a slight feeling of lack of fulfillment. The sense of incompleteness, of wanting more, can be a wonderful reminder of your most sacred, most holy incompleteness.

Any little doing-without can be an occasion for interior glances, but if it can benefit someone else at the same time, so much the better. When you contribute to charity, for example, gently explore the edges of the old saying "Give until it hurts." When you take something away from yourself, consider whether someone else might be in need of it. It should be a completely free and prayerful choice on your part—very different from feeling obliged to take care of everyone else's needs.

You need to keep your motivations clear when you start combining asceticism with charity. Asceticism, as we are describing it here, is practice. You do it to help remember love's presence in the moments of your life. The deepest meaning of charity, however, has nothing to do with practice or personal purposes. Charity *is* love, and truly charitable acts are simply spontaneous expressions of love. So if you give money to the poor as part of your spiritual discipline, try to acknowledge that you are doing it for yourself, not for them. The distinction is important. The poor will understand the difference even if you do not.

It is also important to distinguish between asceticism and habit breaking. Don't confuse fasting with dieting; they are not the same thing. The difference, once again, is in your motivation. What are you really seeking? Is it health and personal improvement, or love and intimacy with God? These motivations need not be mutually exclusive, but neither should they be confused. Take time to reflect prayerfully on the difference. Even if you feel clear about it, proceed prayerfully. Watch out for resolutions and self-manipulations. And whatever you do, don't overdo it. We are looking for gentle reminders, not spiritual gymnastics.

All of us encounter plenty of built-in unsatisfied desires every day. We are always wanting a little something more. We wish we had more money, understanding, or support; we need a new car but can't afford it; we wish our relationships could be more fulfilling, our lives more filled with joy. It is very possible to dedicate such feelings of unfulfillment as remembrances. Then sometimes when you sense a little desire for something you don't have, it may remind you of your great desire for the fullness of what you already have been given. The quaint classical term is *functional asceticism*. It is simply consecrating the natural fastings that are already taking place in daily life.[5]

The contemplative masters knew that all our lives contain a sufficient amount of fasting. Most experimented with extremes of asceticism and then came back to say it was not worth it. The story is told that the Buddha tried all the most severe yoga disciplines of his day but came to enlightenment only after he discovered the Middle Way: not too much, not too little. I know of no contemplative authority who recommended drastic asceticism. Most echo Jesus' advice: seek God in the present moment, and don't worry about tomorrow, because "each day has enough trouble of its own."[6]

Dedicating Pain and Joy

Remember the difference between dedication and consecration. Both involve intention, but dedication means bringing a specific hope or purpose to your experience, while consecration means giving your hope and yourself to God within that experience. In dedication, you designate something as a reminder of God, of your desire for love, or of love's presence around you. In consecration, you consciously offer yourself in hope to the holy One in the midst of your activities. Both are occasions for little interior glances.

There is an old tradition of dedicating one's suffering, whatever it may be, for the sake of others' welfare. Many saints have dedicated their pain in physical illness as a powerful form of intercessory prayer. At the very least, pain can be a reminder of our desire for love and our need for grace. Pain is a fact of life, and although we would rather be without it and should do everything possible to minimize it, we can choose how we wish to be with it.

Any kind of pain can nurture the interior glance. I have known people who were able to let their mental worries or emotional upsets remind them of God in powerful ways. God often reaches us through our distress anyway, but we can join the process with dedication and consecration. It is not always easy, and when the distress is severe, it may seem impossible. But I will never forget one beautiful man who suffered from a deep, crippling depression that had lasted for years and was unresponsive to treatment. In what I consider to be an absolute miracle, he was given the grace to consecrate his suffering entirely: his immobility, his self-disparagement and unreasoning guilt, even his suicidal thoughts. He went far beyond reminders and little glances; his depression was his worship. I have no idea how it was possible, and I have never again seen such a thing. But it did happen, and it could happen again.

In addition to physical pain, then, you might want to ask yourself and God if there are some mental or emotional distresses that call out for dedication or consecration. Do you carry a background worry about your family or your job or your financial situation? Are you sometimes plagued by obsessive thoughts? Do you find yourself frequently concerned about what others think of you, or worried about your performance? Do you have episodes of anxiety? Whatever these unpleasant things may be, might one or more of them be occasions to at least remember your loving desire? Here again we need to try to be clear about our motives. Dedicating a particular discomfort should not be confused with healing. Most important, it should not be a substitute for praying for healing and for medical or psychological care.

In a similar way, you might consider dedicating some of the more pleasant things in your life. A woman I know treasures the short time when she gets home from work. She kicks off her shoes and just relaxes: no demands, no expectations. This is one of the most pleasant regular times of her daily experience, and she found she could dedicate it to God without making it another task. "It's more enjoyable than ever," she said, "because I feel as though I'm sharing it with God. We just hang out together for a while."

An office worker told me in complete seriousness that of all God's creations, she had decided that chocolate and ice cream were the very finest. She remembers God, she says, with every taste of chocolate or ice cream. And chocolate ice cream? "Chocolate ice cream," she said, "is nothing other than heaven." Some things are so good they just dedicate themselves.

In many sweet moments we are reminded of God without even trying. A beautiful sunrise, the birth of a child, the miracle of romantic love: such things are built-in reminders, functional asceticism at its best. At other times of pleasure, however, we tend to focus exclusively on the experience itself, as if we were trying to lose ourselves in it permanently. I am like this with many of the lighter things I enjoy: gentle conversation, good parties with good friends, goofing around with my family, and so on. Afterward, I sometimes marvel at how far away from my mind God has been. It doesn't bother me very much—and I really don't think God minds at all. But when I do remember, a little interior glance in the middle of great, carousing fun is truly beautiful; it is an exchange of little smiles across the room.

When something very nice happens to you or to someone near you, and you come round to celebrating it, there can easily be a double remembrance. One is gratitude to God for the joyful event itself; the other is a simple joining of pleasure. The divine One suffers when we do; so also is the joy shared.

Dedicating Forgetfulness

As you gain experience in the practice of remembering, you will naturally identify the situations and feelings that most interfere with your conscious presence in love. Some will be painfully obvious; you could not ignore them even if you wanted to. Anger is like that for me. Other times of forgetfulness will come to light as you reflect upon your days. For example, I have gradually realized that there are many kinds of anger, and it is one particular form that makes me most forgetful. I can be angered by injustice or irritation and remember God through it all, but when I feel I have a point to make or an ax to grind I become completely forgetful.

When you identify such obstructions, your first reaction will probably be to try to change or eliminate them. As I have advised, the best course of action is simple prayer and gentle awareness. Be cautious about willpower and resolutions; they are likely to become obstacles themselves. Some situations of forgetfulness will disappear as soon as you identify them, as if they were only meant to stay long enough to be recognized. Others will pass away with time, grace, and patience. Still others remain intransigent. But even the most ingrained and entrenched obstacles are susceptible to a little spiritual ambush. You can dedicate them as reminders!

Not long ago a friend and I were talking about our most and least favorite holidays. He said that until recently he had hated Christmas. "I would turn into Scrooge. I'd get into a dulled, hostile state, just doing the next thing, just making it through." Then one day he found himself complaining how Christmas had nothing of Christ in it for so many people, and he realized how true it was for him. "I decided then and there that I was going to let those dazed, angry holiday feelings remind me of the real meaning of Christmas." After that, he said, he began to recover a joy in the holiday that had been absent since his childhood.

One of the daily reflection questions I have suggested is, At what times did I seem most absent, most kidnapped or closed off? As you identify such times, prayerfully consider how the forgetfulness happens and what, if anything, you might do about it. You are likely to notice that your most forgetful times are your most addicted ones: where some attachment has captured you. Do not leap immediately to try to conquer the addiction. We have so many addictions that we could spend all our energy every day of our lives trying to overcome them. Then we would have missed the appreciation of love, and we still would not be free.

Understand this clearly: appreciation of love is not achieved by conquering addictions or by any other kind of self-improvement. It is often the reverse: our most authentic appreciation happens *within* our bondage. God does not wait to come into our lives until we have solved our problems. God is always involved. Love is already here. Be discriminating when you identify an addiction. Some addictions are destructive enough to warrant a real struggle. Others just are not worth it. Do remember, however, that you can sometimes consecrate yourself within an addiction, and you can always dedicate an addiction as a reminder. Then, at the beginning of forgetting, you will remember. You can remember to turn to the source of love as you slip into forgetfulness.

The Ways of Forgetfulness

Look closely at how forgetfulness happens. At first it might seem like a sudden thing; a new thought flashes into consciousness and completely replaces what was there before. But like everything else in the brain and body, forgetting and remembering are transitions. They may happen quickly, but they take long enough to be noticed if you watch with bright, gentle eyes. With some reflection, you can see the transition into forgetfulness happening in two ways.

The first way is losing yourself, sinking into such absorption or dullness that you have no self-awareness at all. It can happen with an activity or relationship in which you become completely preoccupied, or when things are so routine and dull that your whole consciousness goes on automatic pilot. Either way, it is entrancement; you might as well be a robot.

The second way is the opposite; instead of losing your self-awareness, you become self-conscious. This may happen when you are concerned about performance, responsibility, what other people think of you, or whether you are doing things right. Although you are wide awake and not the least bit entranced, you are so self-preoccupied that you forget love's presence entirely.

In my early days of teaching and public speaking, I noticed that as soon as I opened my mouth in such situations, my remembrance of God completely disappeared. For the most part it was self-consciousness, a kind of stage fright. I was so concerned about how I would appear that there was no space for a sense of love. But I also noticed that once I got over my initial self-concern I would become immersed in the discussion, completely entranced by it. I liked the entrancement better than the self-consciousness, but I was even more forgetful of God in it. At least the stage fright, when it was bad enough, had sometimes prompted me to pray, "God, help me get through this." But in the entrancement there was seldom even the smallest interior glance.

When I recognized these two ways of forgetfulness, I dedicated them and began to try to consecrate myself in them. I tagged my self-conscious anxiety as a reminder of God's presence. I remember God at the beginning of every formal talk I give and frequently even when I begin to speak to someone informally. Now I welcome the anxiety; it encourages my prayerfulness and willingness to be vulnerably present. When self-consciousness reappears, it seldom traps me. Instead, it feels like something in me stretching; it is an occasion to yield once again into trust. The entrancement is more difficult, because it is by definition a loss of present-centered awareness. Even so, the beginning feeling of it is now a reminder for me. When I do notice it, I turn to God instead of fighting the entrancement. It is really quite a beautiful experience.

Be always gentle in seeking remembrance; do not make too much of a struggle of it. In the same way that fighting addictions can become an addiction, struggling against forgetfulness can become a source of forgetfulness. Look for the light rather than fighting the darkness. Seek love directly rather than doing battle with the things that distract you from love. Practice presence instead of worrying about all the ways in which you are absent. Hope to remember instead of trying not to forget. Think about it; there is a very real and wonderful difference.

We are seeking fidelity here, not perfection. Look softly, even with compassion, at the things that preoccupy you. Perhaps there are undiscovered possibilities for the little interior glance within them. And it may well be that God is seeking a little conscious connection right there in the midst of your forgetfulness, glancing toward you while you feel so far away.

Prodigal Mind

When our hearts are consecrated and all-inclusive, it does not matter what we are doing, and the thought of God or the remembrance of love need not be in our minds all the time. Everything is simply appreciated lovingly; everything is sacred simply because it is God's creation. But when our hearts are forgotten and our minds caught up in either/or distinctions, we slip away from home like the prodigal son. Our minds go off to some new land and there become rich with thoughts and worries. And, like the prodigal, we keep glancing back over our shoulders, wondering if home is still there. When the time comes for us to recognize our impoverishment, we do return home, and the welcome is always warm.

When we are captured by self-consciousness, entrancement, or dullness, our glances are often nothing more than wistful peeks over our shoulders toward home. It makes us homesick, and that is good. At other times the glance is liberating; in a flash it breaks the chains of our compulsiveness. We think home is a long way off, but when we glance toward it we are suddenly there. It may last only a moment before we are captured again, but we have seen that home is all around us, right where we are, in the midst of everything that is going on. It is only grace that makes the difference between wistful longing and immediate realization. All we can do is feel our homesickness and glance hopefully toward the source of love.

Our intentional reminders are just ways of glancing homeward. Classically, they are called "aids to recollection" or "sacramentals." Before I learned the religious words, I called them gimmicks. Call them what you like, and let your spirit run free with them. Experiment with them; play around with them; try being serious; explore being foolish. You may find ways and means that last for a long time, or you may need to change your approach every day. There is no one right way, except the one that fits the shape of your heart in this moment. Just don't make them too important. They are ways of looking homeward; they are not home itself.

Notice the reminders that are already a natural part of your life. Enjoy and encourage them. As for new inspirations, try just one or two at the outset, and ask God to help guide your choices. Keep it simple. When you find or are given something that sprouts a good crop of interior glances, savor it for as long as it lasts. But don't hold on. Most reminders will become stale at some point. You will become so used to them, so habituated, that they lose their awakening quality. Then it is time for something fresh or, God willing, time for nothing special at all.[7]

Most of all, look for the little gifts that each day brings. Whenever a sound stops, pause for just a moment in the silence, and just be in love. When you are going from one place to another, *do* stop to smell the flowers. Notice what the sky looks like, where the sun and moon are. Really *see* the people you pass. When you park your car and turn off the motor, take a moment to look and listen before you jump out and rush to your errands. When you're taking a bath or a shower, listen for a little while after you turn off the water. When you have been very active and sit down to rest, don't just immediately collapse into dullness. Stretch a little, and yield into presence. As you are going to sleep or waking up, do it with God in mind. Such little moments, occasioned by virtually anything that sparks your attention, are like precious sips of water in the deserts of daily activity. And there are so very many of them, if we would only stop to notice.

8

THE PRAYER OF THE HEART

A naked intent toward God, the desire for God alone, is
enough. If you want to gather all your desire into one simple word, choose a short word rather than a long one.
Then fix it in your mind so that it will remain there come
what may.

THE CLOUD OF UNKNOWING

The second of Brother Lawrence's four ways of practice is simple; one keeps a prayer going on inside all the time, no matter
what. It has been called perpetual prayer, habitual prayer, constant prayer, or the prayer of the heart. Prehistoric people probably prayed in this fashion. Recitation of mantras, sacred syllables
or phrases repeated silently or aloud, was evident in Hindu practice thousands of years ago and became an integral part of early
Buddhist spirituality. In Christianity, the "Jesus prayer" was in
place as early as the fourth century, and in Islamic Sufism the
practice of constantly reciting the names of God was apparent in
the eighth century.[1]

I will speak primarily of the Christian version, because it is
what I know best. Beginning in the early days of Christian desert
asceticism in the third and fourth centuries, men and women
sought to dedicate their entire attention to prayerfulness. They
wanted to put Saint Paul's command to pray constantly into true
practice. They struggled for years to keep their hearts centered in
God, and they discovered practical ways of helping this happen.

Ever since, there has been a tradition of dedicated heart prayer in Christianity. From the early desert, the practice developed into the tradition known as Hesychasm (from the Greek *hesuchia,* meaning quiet). It became primarily associated with Eastern Orthodox spirituality in writings such as the *Philokalia,* but it has also had a strong effect upon the Western church. The four-teenth-century *Cloud of Unknowing* is a Western spiritual classic that describes the practice in great detail.[2]

For the most part, practices of continuous prayer have involved steady repetition of a word or a phrase, with the attempt to keep it going within one's awareness no matter what else may be happening. With sufficient repetition, the prayer becomes a natural part of oneself, truly a prayer of the heart.

In old biblical understanding, the heart did not refer specifi-cally to the blood-pumping organ we think of nowadays. Nor was its meaning limited to the emotion of love. Instead, the heart was viewed as the center of the person, where one's deep-est desires and convictions abide. In later spiritual thought, the heart center also came to be understood as the place where we are in most intimate contact with God's presence and with our essential union with others, where the deep, ongoing love affair between God and human beings actually takes place.

The oldest forms of Christian heart prayer were probably short verses from the psalms. One phrase that was repeated in the very early days of the Christian desert tradition was "God make haste to help me" from Psalm 22. By the fourth century, empha-sis was being placed on invoking the name of Jesus, and monks were sometimes advised simply to center all their concentration on this name alone. A very widely used form was the plea of the blind Bartimaeus from Mark 10: "Jesus, son of David, have pity on me." Later, this became associated with the famous tax col-lector's prayer from Luke 18: "God be merciful to me, a sinner." Over generations, these forms were blended together into the most widely known Christian heart prayer, the Jesus prayer: "Lord Jesus Christ, Son of God, have mercy upon me, a sinner."

Many modern people who might otherwise feel drawn to this ancient form of prayer are put off by its emphasis on sinfulness. In contemporary Christian spirituality there is a strong movement toward reclaiming our inherent goodness as God's children and deemphasizing the heaviness of original sin and human defectiveness. If this is of concern to you, it may be important to know two things about the history of the Jesus prayer. First, as I indicated above, the word *sinner* was not in the earliest forms of the prayer, and when it was introduced it referred not to an essential badness of persons but to "missing the mark" as all of us are bound to do. Second, in modern religious usage we tend to associate mercy only with the judgment of God, as if we were criminals facing the last judgment and throwing ourselves on the mercy of a court. But the classical meaning of mercy (*chanan* in Hebrew, or *eleeo* in Greek) is much wider in scope; it means kindness, graciousness, loving helpfulness.

It is solid traditional theology to believe that human beings are inherently good and beautiful because we are God's children. We are made in God's image and carry God's love in us as the most essential part of our nature. An ancient talmudic expression is, "And be not wicked in thine own sight." A popular modern way of saying it is, "God don't make junk."[3]

Yet we are also sinful; we are in many ways mistaken, deluded, addicted, estranged, and unloving. And I am convinced that sometimes, for no other reason than nastiness, we are just downright mean. We are all both saints and sinners. But regardless of how we think about ourselves, love is the source of our life, and only grace enables our living into greater fullness of love. In this sense the Jesus prayer in its longest form applies to every conceivable situation in which we might find ourselves and every possible self-image we might entertain. It is as meaningful in joyful, beautiful, laughing moments as in times of sorrow or painful self-recognition.

But the Jesus prayer is by no means the only prayer of the heart. *The Cloud of Unknowing* suggested taking any word or short phrase that symbolized God and to concentrate on it, avoiding all other thoughts. In a related practice, Simone Weil, the French mystical writer of the early twentieth century, recited the Lord's Prayer silently in Greek with what she called perfect attention. In contemporary times, some variations of popular "centering prayer" or "breath prayer" have become prayers of the heart.

Finding a Heart Prayer

The basic practice of heart prayer involves selecting a word, phrase, or image and planting it deeply within yourself during times of formal prayer and meditation. Then, during the rest of the day, you can notice it going on inside in the midst of all your activities.

Note that I said you could use an image as well as a word or a phrase. Nearly all traditional descriptions of heart prayer prescribe the use of words, but some people find a mental or visual image much more helpful. After you have had some experience with this form of prayer, you might explore the possibilities of more subtle forms: sounds, body sensations, inner feelings, even the simple, bare sense of your longing; all can be prayers of the heart. Over time, you can experiment to see what form of heart prayer seems most right for you, but at the beginning I suggest you stay with one prayer for a week or two before changing it. Give it time to grow deep inside you, and see what happens as it does.

To select a prayer, you can follow the advice of the *Cloud of Unknowing;* just choose a short word that somehow "gathers your desire." Examples include Love, Trust, God, Yahweh,

Yeshua, Christ, Jesus, Shalom, Peace. The deeper, more prayerful way of finding a heart prayer is to ask God to give it to you. This would be the best heart prayer, I think—one that comes from your heart and represents the deep, wordless prayer that has been going on inside you all along. To use Brother Lawrence's words, let love inspire it. Just make the request and then be still, watching for what seems to be given: a word, phrase, image, or feeling that comes into your awareness spontaneously. If something comes and has a right kind of feeling about it, do not worry about whether it has been divinely inspired or whether you have conjured it up yourself. Just gently turn it and caress it a little. Does it deepen your presence, or pull you away? Does it inspire trust, or fear? Does it represent love, or alienation, willingness, or willfulness? If it simply seems more wrong than right, go back to the source and ask to return it in exchange for another.

The *Cloud* recommends a one-syllable word, but I think there is no problem with making it a little longer. Just keep it simple. Don't start out with something as intricate as Simone Weil's Lord's Prayer in Greek. The idea is to have a prayer going on within you that you can notice at any time. If it is too long or complicated, noticing it will require too much effort. All or part of the Jesus prayer would be fine, or a line or two from scripture or a hymn, or a simple image such as light or a symbol of your faith.

Practicing Heart Prayer

In your set-aside prayer time, after you've done what you need to settle down and orient yourself toward the source of love, allow the heart prayer to start within you. If it is made of words, let it begin in the same gentle way that any other easy thought might start; then allow it to repeat itself over and over. If it is an image, let it be in your awareness gently, like a memory. If you sense things easily, you might entertain a notion of physically planting the prayer like a seed in your heart or the center of your being, gently, softly, tenderly. The prayer of the heart requires a light and delicate touch; ideally, it should be completely effortless.

It takes some practice to just let the prayer continue gently in your awareness. You should not be trying to concentrate on the prayer; it needs to be within you while everything else is going on, not to the exclusion of anything. This means you need to be very easeful, remaining attentive to the prayer but neither holding on to it nor shutting out other things. This kind of gentle attentiveness is something that comes only with graced experience, and it is one of the reasons set-aside time is so important for this practice.

The best way to cultivate effortless, gentle attentiveness is to adopt a very permissive attitude toward your mind. Let your mind do what it wants; don't struggle with it. This will probably take some getting used to, because most of us are accustomed to trying to make our unruly minds behave. If you approach your mind with notions of effortful concentration, you are likely only to create further noise and disruption. Instead, be very tender and patient with your thoughts, not worried by what you might consider to be distractions. Remember that you are not alone in this endeavor; there is no need to strive.

With this permissive attitude, you will find yourself attending to the prayer for a while, and then some other thoughts or images will capture your attention and take you away. Don't try to prevent this from happening, but when you notice that you have been carried off somewhere, bring your attention gently back to the prayer. Similarly, you will probably notice dullness or sleepiness creeping in at times. Again, don't try to keep it from happening, but when you notice it, take a breath or two and gently reawaken. If you find yourself struggling to concentrate on the prayer or to keep it in mind, it is time to relax. The heart prayer is like presence in love itself; you cannot successfully maintain it without interruption, but you can come home to it whenever you notice that you have gone away.

Once again, give up all concerns about success and failure. What you are doing in these times of formal meditation is planting the prayer within yourself so that it will be there through the rest of the day. It is indeed very much like planting a seed in the ground. You just put it there and let it take its natural course. Don't keep digging it up to see how it is growing. Don't try to manipulate it or control it; just notice it, appreciate it. Entrust its care to God. You may find that the prayer wants to change, to move to slightly different words or images. If it seems to be changing into something that is more helpful, let it do so. There is no reason to hold on to it rigidly.

Stay with this prayerful practice for as long as is comfortable. Then, when it's time to go on about your business, be sure to feather out the transition. Ask God to keep the heart prayer going within you. Notice the prayer inside you as you move into your next activity. Then, during the rest of the day, whenever you remember, just notice the prayer happening inside. Sometimes it will come into your awareness all by itself. At other times one of your reminders will cause you to notice it. But if you plant it gently and attend to it with open diligence, you will realize the prayer is happening whether you are noticing it or not; it is just going on, all by itself. Just as we are in love whether we know it or not, something in your heart is praying constantly even when your mind is captured by something else. Brother Lawrence would say that something in us is in constant prayer whether we practice a heart prayer or not. He would say that this intentional use of a word, phrase, or image is simply making the ongoing dialogue with God more conscious.

Breath as Heart Prayer

As I have said, breath is the most common symbol of spirit, and it is always with us as a reminder of our presence in love. Because of its rhythmic, repetitive nature, breath is also ideally suited as an aid to heart prayer. If the heart prayer is made of words, people often find it spontaneously repeating itself in time with their breathing. Because of this experience, a variety of breath prayers has emerged. One ancient suggestion was to use the name of Jesus as the heart prayer, and to repeat it with every in-breath and out-breath. Another was based on the Jesus prayer; on breathing in, "Lord Jesus Christ," and on breathing out, "Have mercy upon me." For many years, a friend of mine has breathed "Love" and "Trust."

Any form of heart prayer can be associated with breathing. Even images, especially if they are simple, can find a connection with the breath. One can, for example, entertain an image of breathing the light of God in and out. Or one might picture the cross of Christ within one's heart and breathe in and out to and from that place. In the most ancient Christian tradition, the heart was metaphorically considered the center of the body, located in the abdomen. A common instruction was "put your mind in your heart," which literally meant to attend to one's belly, to watch the stomach rise and fall as the name of Jesus was recited with the breath. It is where "contemplating your navel" came from.

The association of heart prayer with breath is something that happens spontaneously, and should not be forced or contrived. If your heart prayer seems to find a connection with your breathing, just let it develop. Your breathing is natural; so should your prayer be. The whole idea of heart prayer is not to contrive prayerfulness but to come closer to the utterly natural prayer that is already going on within us. Consciously repeated prayers are surface reflections of the great unconscious prayer: the one to which Brother Lawrence referred when he said we would be surprised by what our souls say to God. An eighth-century Hindu text describes the inaudible sound that is every human being's natural breath prayer. The breath silently says "hahm" coming in and "sah" going out, all by itself. It "sounds in every living being spontaneously every moment without any conscious effort."[4]

Some Cautions

Because heart prayer may involve more active intention than simple remembering, it can take us more deeply into the confusing territory of desire, intention, and control. As it was originally practiced, the prayer of the heart required great concentration— much more effort than I have suggested. The sacred word or phrase was used as the center of attention, and all other sensations and activities of the mind were considered to be distractions. It was a real struggle for control. Such effortful concentration produces an inevitable battle within the praying person for control of attention, an attempt to focus on the prayer and not be kidnapped by other thoughts or sensations. It encourages resolutions and willful control; it produces a kind of warfare within oneself.

Such interior battling can become an attempt to focus on God to the exclusion of everything else. Indeed, that was precisely the intent in the early Hesychast tradition. It made a certain sense in those days when people felt a great disparity between body, mind, and soul, and considered temptations of the flesh to be demonic. "A lover of God," said Basil the Great, "flees all things and goes to God."[5]

But in modern times it does not make sense to try to shut out the world in order to become more loving. Certainly it was not Brother Lawrence's intent to exclude the world by attending to

God. On the contrary, he intended the little phrase that love inspires to be a means of coming *into* the world from the center point of God. That is why he emphasized that the prayer should be inspired by love. To be fair, the old-time world-deniers were also doing it for love. Whether or not they ever realized an all-encompassing presence of love, they never doubted that charity was the greatest virtue, and they sought always to deepen love in the world. They just didn't want the world to get in their way while they were doing it.

So do keep a gentle touch on things. Let your eyes be soft when you see, your ears be tender as you hear, your hands be delicate as you touch, your mind be merciful as you proceed. If you find yourself working hard at this kind of prayer, trying to hold on to something or flee from something, it is time to relax and turn homeward to the grace of God once more. Cultivate an openness of attitude. Find your personal power and strength in desire and consecration, not in manipulation. Take the time to stretch and yield. Seek an all-embracing presence. When you find yourself struggling to shut something out, ease up and let it be. You don't need to make *anything* the center of attention. As long as your attentiveness springs forth from the ground of your desire for love, your center of attention can be everywhere and nowhere at the same time.

Embracing Presence

Remember also that any prayer you might say consciously is but a wave on the surface of the great prayer being prayed deeply in you by the source of love every moment of your life. Remembering the mystery of God's presence with us, which is at once immanent, transcendent, and all-pervasive, it is obvious that we cannot be attending to the true presence of God if we are focusing solely on a word, phrase, or image. At the very best, these are only symbolic reflections and expressions of God's presence and our desire. In moments of sheer grace, the symbols become icons: windows that give us a glimpse into the all-pervading presence of God's love. But always they are the means, not the end.

We can test any practice of prayer by seeing how it assists us in being more present to other people and to situations as well as being more present to God. This requires us to cut through some of our old images of God. Our minds like to put reality in compartments, with God there and we here and the rest of the world somewhere else. Sometimes we just have to remind ourselves that God's presence is not reserved for any particular space. Though we may be more aware of God's presence in one place than in another, we need to remember that wherever we look, wherever our attention goes, God is there.

If God's presence is indeed everywhere, then it makes no sense to try to be present to God only in some sacred spot away from distractions. In heart prayer especially, though, we are liable to try to withdraw into the privacy of our own interior to find God. If we do this excessively, we are likely to start thinking that God is only "in here," and that the world "out there" is devoid of God's presence.

To counteract this tendency, we need to realize that what we call distractions are not the things themselves but the way our attention becomes absorbed in them, the way we are captured by them. Distractions are completely determined by our attachments. Think about hearing the sounds of children playing. If we are in an open, easy state of mind the sounds are like music. But if we are trying to concentrate on something else, the sounds are distractions; they are noise instead of music. It is all in the mind; our attachments make the decision for us.

As another example, consider the difference between flowers and weeds. If you are invested in keeping your lawn just right, a dandelion growing there is a weed. But when a child picks that very same blossom and brings it to you as a gift, it suddenly becomes a flower. Flowers are plants that grow where we want them to grow; weeds are plants growing against our will. It is the same with distractions; distractions are the noise and weeds of our minds. If our attachments could just shift a little, what were distractions could become music and flowers.

In the context of practicing love's presence, distractions are simply the result of our focusing attention on something to the extent that we ignore God's presence. They are not to be fought off by trying to exclude them by focusing our attention on God. Instead, our attention needs to open, to become more easeful and all-inclusive. In such openness we need be forgetful neither of God nor of God's creation. Only in this way can we even begin to move toward fulfillment of the two great commandments: loving God with our whole hearts and loving others as ourselves. Once again, the openness is only a grace we can pray for and be willing to receive. We cannot willfully dispense with our attachments, so we are bound to feel distracted.

Simply remember that being present to God and practicing loving presence somehow lead us to greater openness to the world as well. Especially in the practice of the prayer of the heart, don't work at focusing your attention. If distractions occur, don't try to shut them out forcefully. Relax the either-or distinctions that your mind is bound to make, and pray for a greater both-and awareness. Let your attention move back and forth between prayer and distraction with gentleness and smoothness. Be gracefully flexible.

9

LOVING THE SOURCE OF LOVE

O women of the city,
Swear by the wild field doe
Not to wake or rouse us
Till we fulfill our love.
THE SONG OF SONGS

Whether we are distracted or not, whether we know it or not, whether we even *want* it or not, a communication between the soul and God keeps going on beneath the surface of our self-awareness. It is given, everywhere and at all times. There is no need to attain it; there is nothing we have to do to make it happen. Neither can we escape from it. In the psalmist's words, "Where can I flee from your presence? If I take the wings of the morning and dwell beyond the sea, even there your hand will guide me, your right hand will hold me."[1]

Relationship with the source of love is the most natural thing about us. Active practice of this relationship is nothing other than living, as best we can, in appreciation of and fidelity to the continual heart-to-heart connectedness with the holy Other whose presence makes us complete. Brother Lawrence called it conversing everywhere with God.

The great majority of religious people have some notion of relationship to God, but most do not recognize it as the birthright of all human beings. They see it instead as a supernatural event: an extraordinary breakthrough of heaven into human life. Regardless of how it is viewed, however, relationship with God is the most common way people practice the presence of love.

It is also the most thorny, sensitive, and potentially disruptive way. What kind of relationship do I think I have with God, or God with me? Is my God male or female, mother or father, friend or lover, companion or master, protector or challenger, ruler or servant, critical judge or laughing dancing partner? What if I were indeed to fly into morning or dwell beyond the sea; would God really be there? And what will happen if I come too close to God? Can I be truly loving and survive, or will God's flaming passion consume me until there is nothing left?

Those are just some of the questions I have had to face; you can add your own if you dare. Does it have to be so complicated? Yes, I think for most of us it does. A few blessed souls are graced with childlike simplicity in love throughout their lives. The rest of us must seek the simplicity beneath, within, and beyond a host of complications. We can do our best not to add anything extra, but we do have to face what we encounter. And whatever else it may be, relationship is encounter.

Little glances and repetitive prayers can be loving, sweet, and deep, but it is in practicing direct relationship with God that we encounter the grits and guts of love. Here are the breadth and depth of personal joy and pain, consolation and desolation, reassurance and fear, communion and alienation. Here are the flesh and bones of love's invitation. Saying yes commits us to a certain trouble. With gentle ease or gulping apprehension, we must feel the practice is worth it.

The possibilities for practice are endless. I will discuss three common ways as examples: companionship, romance, and cosmic presence. Then I will suggest some reflections that might help you discern your own invitations. It is not a matter of shopping around for a sense of relationship. A way—or more likely several ways at once—are given, called for, waiting to emerge.

Companionship

The most common sense of relationship is one in which God is seen as a loving companion. Long ago the psalmists sang of God's abiding presence. Throughout the Christian Gospels, Jesus keeps inviting people to follow him, take him in, keep him company, and love him. "I shall not call you servants any more," he said, "I call you friends." In more recent Christianity, hymns like "Just a Closer Walk with Thee," "What a Friend We Have in Jesus," and "Jesus Loves Me" have been integral parts of worship. The most popular prayers contain phrases like "The Lord be with you" or "Lord, be present with us here today." If you were to take such prayers literally they would be heretical; the words assume God might *not* be with us. I prefer to look more kindly at the prayers, as shorthand ways of saying, "God, help us to be at least a little bit as present with you as you are present with us."[2]

Children develop a sense of the divine Person as friend very easily, and we adults may consider it childish to have a friendly relationship with God. It can sound too much like having an imaginary playmate. But if a casual, friendly sense of God does come to us sometimes, we might be wise not to cast it aside too quickly. To walk along a shore with God, to play hide-and-seek, to giggle and hold God's hand might not be infantile luxuries. Jesus, for one, said there was no way to enter the reign of heaven "unless you change and become like little children."[3]

Children readily associate the companionship of God with the best of human parenting. Seeing God as parent may also seem childish. But might there be, in the unadmitted sparkle of the child within you, a sometime longing to climb into God's fatherly lap, to nestle against God's motherly breast, to rest for a moment in the shadow of God's wings or be held in God's strong and tender arms? If you could allow yourself to feel it, are there not times when you would love to cry on God's shoulder, to let God tell you you are worthwhile and beautiful? And is there not something in you that would be delighted if you could bring a smile to God's face?

Please dispense with your maturity for a moment and indulge yourself. Do not be concerned with psychology, theology, or right or wrong. Direct relationship with God is the one place where you can be absolutely trusting of your desire and give it full reign. You will never know how safe the place is until you risk being in it fully. No hesitation is called for, nor even any discernment. And though you may be afraid, there is no need to be. Here you are not only in God's unconditional embrace, but also in the good company of saints who snuggled with God, of psalmists who were free to be selfish with God, of prophets who argued with God, of Jesus who loved to call God "Daddy."[4]

When you must be more dignified, or when it is right to recognize the majestic transcendence of the divine One, do not jump immediately to prescribed methods. See what seems to be invited. Try a little dialogue with God, in your heart or in spoken or written words. Look around for what might already be given in the realms of feeling, thinking, and action. Consider the companionship between God and persons in healing, justice seeking, peacemaking, and cocreation.

The most reverent sense of companionship is an "I-Thou" appreciation that permits loving intimacy while preserving the sacred distinction between person and God. It is free from restriction by any particular images of God or self; it does not make an object of either party. It is free yet committed, reverent yet full of intimate mutuality. According to Martin Buber, it can become the deepest kind of relationship, a realization that God needs us as much as we need God.[5]

At first, the idea of God's needing us may seem to breach the doctrine of God's omnipotence. If God not only desires our love but actually needs and depends upon it, does that not weaken God's inherent power? The answer lies in where the need comes from. Yes, God has needs. But God's needs come from love, and love is free. God does not love us out of need, but needs us because of love. It is absolute, unconditional, and totally free love. God is hurt by our absence from the play of love—the spirit of love is diminished when we turn away from it—but God chooses to be willing to let us go and to suffer the diminishment.[6]

In their own experience of life and prayer, contemplatives have consistently discovered that the source of love does indeed need us, for the continuing process of creation and for the sake of love as an end in itself. God is pleased and made happy by us and deeply desires to make us happy. God needs us as someone to love and someone to be loved by. The love can take many forms; it may be severe, tender, wistful, intimate, passionate. It can be expressed in action, stillness, words, silence, thoughts, feelings. Sometimes it is felt and expressed in ways that are undeniably sexual: yearning, embracing, excitement, fulfillment, and resting so deep and physical that one can never again doubt the fullness of divine incarnation.

Romance

If you have not already done so, read the beautiful collection of love poems called the Song of Songs. It is not long, and it is erotic enough to hold anyone's interest. We never studied it in Sunday school at the little midwestern Methodist church of my childhood. It never appeared as scripture for the day. Not a single sermon was preached about it. But we were in good company; a talmudic tradition says there was great debate nearly two thousand years ago as to whether the book should be included in the Jewish canon of scripture, and some people were even "excluded from the resurrection" for singing its verses at weddings.[7]

The poetry probably originated as love songs in Palestine in the fifth or fourth century B.C. Some say it is an allegory of the love between God and Israel. Others cite it as the best scriptural expression of romance between the individual soul and God. Although it was written long before the time of Christ, many Christian authorities see it as depicting the Church's relationship with God.

Whatever its original intent, the Song of Songs is among the most beautiful love poetry ever written, and mystics through the centuries have found in it words and images to express their own experience of falling in love with God. Many wrote their own versions and commentaries. Origen, Gregory of Nyssa, Bernard of Clairvaux, Mechtilde of Magdeburg, John of the Cross, and Teresa of Avila are just a few who did so. A story about Teresa's commentary is typical of her delightful personality. Her confessor ordered her to burn her manuscript because he felt it was dangerous for a woman to write of such things. Ever obedient, she immediately tossed it into the fire. She knew what he did not: many of her friends had copies of it.

When romance with God happens, companionship changes from gentle longing or dedicated worship and service into an absolutely passionate love affair. God is no longer only friendly companion or majestic holy Other; now the source of love is the one great lover. Arbitrary lines between spirituality and sexuality disappear. Although hints of romance with God are experienced by everyone who practices love's presence, full erotic passion is less common. Of the people who have confided to me in depth, less than half have had such feelings.

In some cases people are too fearful to let the feelings come to consciousness, but I also assume it is just not God's way for many people. Romantic passion is but one of many ways of loving God. It may appear dramatic and enticing, but it might not be what love is inviting. Never assume that your spiritual life is less deep or valuable because it seems less colorful than someone else's. Evelyn Underhill, the great twentieth-century student of spiritual passion, put it strongly: "Do not make the mistake of thinking if you feel cold and dead, that you do not know how to love." The question is not whether one way is better or more attractive than another. The question is what God is inviting.[8]

When God does invite romance, the courtship holds more agony as well as more joy than any human love affair ever could. Contemplative writers struggle and barely begin to express the wounds and ravishings of divine love, the sickness unto death that unabashed passion with God can bring. In a prison cell in sixteenth-century Spain, John of the Cross wrote his version of the Song of Songs. In stanzas of impeccable beauty, John described how God had wounded him with love, stolen his heart, and left him "dying of ah, I don't know what." *"Mas, ¿Cómo perseveras, Oh vida, no viviendo donde vives,"* John cries. (How do you endure, O life, not living where you live?) *¿Por qué, pues has llagado aqueste corazón, no le sanaste?"* (Why, since You wounded this heart, don't You heal it?)[9]

What can be done with such feelings? When the passion for God becomes physically painful, when spiritual yearning becomes absolutely sexual, where does one turn? The natural response is to try to find union with another person. It is no accident, I think, that many lovers of God fall into illicit human love affairs. Spiritual seekers seek one another, and if it happens that two people who are trying to bear the beams of God's passionate love are sexually attracted to each other, it is not an easy thing. There is a kind of sexual addiction, I think, the roots of which are to be found in passionate love for God.

It is also no accident that passionate lovers of God may become addicted to food, work, alcohol or other drugs, or extremes of asceticism. The words of John of the Cross are not simple, empty prettiness. They describe a yearning so fierce that at times one might consider doing anything to ease it. Any outlet, any anesthesia might seem worth a try. It is said that Origen, perhaps the foremost Christian theologian of the third century, finally castrated himself when he had to work with young female converts.[10]

But there can finally be no outlet, no anesthesia, no self-inflicted way of ending the pain. The beams of love must be borne. No human love affair can substitute for the divine one; no drug or food will really fill the emptiness; no overwork or preoccupation can finally overshadow the yearning; no ascetical extremes can stop the pain. There is no way out—only through. As the poetry of John of the Cross so vividly attests, the wound of love must remain open until God heals it. It is God's way of drawing every hidden "no," "maybe," or "yes but" into one completely joyous, unreserved "YES!" It is love's way of becoming everything.

Can such a thing be practiced? Amazingly, it can. But romance with God makes clear how we must understand what all practice really means. No romance, human or divine, can ever be achieved; if it happens, it happens. It is given. This is obvious in romance, but it applies to all practices, all ways of

seeking deeper presence in love. As consecration in action, practice is our expression of desire and willingness for what love
gives and invites. It is our dedicated availability, our wakeful
responsiveness, our fidelity in hope. If we truly understand what
practice means, we can practice anything. Let me give two
examples of practicing romance with God.

The first way involves encountering our feelings toward God
as directly and honestly as possible. It is an active willingness to
experience not only our longings but our fears and whatever
other true emotions we have. We can pray for this openness, and
in moments when we have a choice, we can try to welcome our
feelings instead of shutting them out.

Some people are more naturally in touch with feelings than
others. It might be assumed that they are more likely to experience romance with God, but I do not think that is true. I have
seen the most unfeeling people suddenly, passionately fall in love
with God, and the most sentimental folks gently pulled away
from their emotions toward calm and studied relationship. Such
examples put the lie to theories that propose our relationships
with God are psychologically predictable. God calls the human
heart in God's own way. God knows how or why.

I am sure God does call each of us according to our uniqueness, but only God knows what that uniqueness is. In all things
that have to do with love, we must remain open to being surprised. So for God's sake, if you are surprised by romantic feelings, erotic images, or sexual arousal in the midst of prayer, try
not to flee in fear. All of us need healing from the old severance
of body from spirit; pray for the grace to allow it to happen.

A second way of practicing romance with God is to relax our
defenses against loving and being loved by one another, to
stretch and to yield ourselves more into interpersonal love. Love
is so uncontrollable that we all have many internal defenses

against it. For the same reason, society places rigid external limitations on how love should be expressed. We call it propriety. Even the ancient bride of the Song of Songs struggled with social convention. "If only you were my brother," she cried, "then I could kiss you without people thinking ill of me!"[11]

Most of us do not even approach the limits of social propriety, much less break the law. We are too afraid of pain, guilt, and the unknown, too restricted within ourselves. Our restraint may keep us out of trouble, but it may also keep us from loving enough. I do not encourage you to engage in illicit loving, nor the licit but addicted loving of codependence. But I do encourage you to let yourself love and be loved according to the invitations of your prayer. Test your perceptions with others, with the scripture and moral principles of your faith, but do not run away. Do not let fear rule you; seek the light. Stretch and yield.

Even the most passionate romantic love does not need to be blind. Surely it contains much confusion, and the guideposts are often unclear and difficult to follow. But you can know the difference between the drivenness of fear and the drawingness of love, you can know what it is to be willing to trust God's mercy, and you can know that the inevitable pains of love are worth it.

And, if you are honest with yourself, you can sense at least something of where you are on the spectrum between unconditional love and addicted dependence or codependence. The more addicted love is, the more choiceless and enslaving it feels and the more powerless and demeaned you feel within it. The more unconditional love is, the more free it feels and the more empowered and worthwhile you feel within it. The differences are clear in the abstract, but the experience is always a blending, a matter of degree. Only God's love for the people of love is without conditions, completely unaddicted.

In practice, then, to stretch and yield into interpersonal love is to risk greater attachment, to dance along the edges of dependence and sometimes fall over. It is not to seek more addiction than we already have, but to risk that it might happen and to be willing to bear the pain of withdrawal and our abject dependence upon God's grace in the addictions we do stumble into. Do not contrive anything, but if the invitation is more to love than to safety, choose love. Let yourself love God, other people, and God-in-other-people even if you feel unable or afraid of being hurt; let yourself be loved by God, other people, and God-in-other-people even if you feel unworthy or afraid of being overwhelmed. A few days before her death in 1906, Elizabeth of the Trinity wrote a note to the prioress of her Carmelite monastery. In it, she kept repeating a phrase that could well be a call to everyone: "Let yourself be loved ... LET yourself be loved ... *LET* yourself be loved ..."[12]

You may feel there are too many people to love and be loved by—that more loving would be hopeless complication. Or you may feel there is no one to love or to love you. Either way, it is not your business to make loving happen. Only be willing, open, stretching and yielding into what is given. *Let* it happen, where and when and as it will. And pray.

Cosmic Presence

The third example of relationship is, in a way, even more intimate than romance. It is the sense of God as cosmic presence and of love surrounding, embracing, pervading ourselves and all creation. It might at first seem impossible to have a sense of relationship without a more solid image of the source of love. But it is very possible. To use Martin Buber's terms, it happens when I-It becomes I-You and finally I-Thou. It is revealed in the Hindu greetings *jai bhagwan* and *namaste* that reverence the divinity that both resides within and embraces us all. Indeed, some people find all images restrictive to their sense of the holy.[13]

A child's first sense of life is probably like this all-encompassing presence; only later do personal images of the divine One begin to form. Although the images help in thinking and talking about God, they can sometimes become idols, substituting themselves for the holy Mystery they represent. There is a tendency in all of us to try to domesticate the source of love, to bring God's awesome reality down to a more manageable form, and we use our images to do this.

Thus many people find that a relatively imageless awareness of God is not only more authentic in their experience but also theologically more faithful to the essence of God "in whom we live and move and have our being." God's presence is then the atmosphere that births and embraces all of creation, the Spirit of Christ "filling the cosmos," the eternal "I Am That I Am." As such, the mysterious presence of the divine can be in active relationship with people, calling us, moving us, inspiring us, loving us and desiring our love in return, and all the while remaining unrestricted by our minds.[14]

This form of relationship is practiced primarily through reverence, awe, and wonder. Remembering the divine presence in all things, noticing evidences of it, marveling at the bare fact of life, reveling in the pulse of creation and in love's dynamic pervasiveness: all are occasions for appreciation, praise, and thanksgiving. Such appreciations are stretches of the heart, reaching toward the wonder and opening to the mystery. Once again, yielding follows stretching. Here the yielding is conscious acknowledgment of the great cosmic process of life, welcoming and joining the living flow of love. It is giving oneself into the mystery and allowing the mystery *of* oneself to participate in endless graceful surprise.

If you find yourself encountered by such mystery, be hospitable. Welcome the imageless presence instead of immediately trying to identify or label it. Let yourself be simply appreciative without comprehension. Welcome mystery into yourself; look for awe; recover childlike wonder. Spend a while looking into the night sky or at the petals of a flower. Marvel at the simple fact of being, the amazing reality of just being conscious. You think thoughts, feel feelings, sense perceptions: how incredible!

Discerning Ways of Relationship

The three examples I have given demonstrate a range of possibilities of relationship with the divine. Each has its truth; none is complete. There is no right way, only that which love is inviting in you at this very moment. If you seek a way of relating to God, you can do no better than to let God come into your awareness as God will. Be open to any possibilities, willing to be surprised. At one moment there may be a very distinct image; at another, an imageless presence; at still another, only the groans of your yearning echoing in emptiness.

Relationship implies participation, and there are many ways we can actively participate without trying to control things. We can pray for a deeper sense of relationship. We can actively seek it by "staying awake, praying at all times." We can also explore our personal histories to discover some little hints about how God and our hearts have been relating all along.[15]

This reflection is important enough to warrant spending some time writing (or drawing if pictures work better for you). The basic questions are, How have you tended to experience God's presence in your life up until now? How do you most naturally relate to God right now? In your most sincere prayer, how do you sense your relationship with the source of love? The idea is to see if there are some themes you can pick up on, some naturally given ways of relatedness that you can encourage and cultivate more intentionally.

Begin with prayer expressing your desire to perceive love's invitations more accurately. Scan over your life and note times that stand out as especially sacred. When have you felt most close to God? If you think you have never felt God's presence, simply reword the question: What have been some of the peak experiences of your life? In what moments have you felt most touched, awestruck, moved, connected, fulfilled, loving, loved, or whole? Ask yourself these questions even if you are very certain of your experiences of God's presence; they may help you recall times that you had not previously connected with God.

Be especially on the lookout for experiences that you would not normally call religious or spiritual. Most of us have made compartments in our lives that we are not fully aware of. For example, we might expect some sense of God in church or in prayer, but not in watching television, doing the laundry, or in anger or boredom. But God refuses to be compartmentalized and may show up in the most surprising places. If you identify such experiences, spend a few moments remembering them. As far as possible, relive the times and notice what it feels like. Make some notes. Don't worry about finding the right words; the notes are just to help your recall later.

Once you have identified some of these times, you can begin a little intellectual and theological reflection. Are there some basic common themes in the experiences, such as peace and trust, passionate desire, or fear and trembling? Is there any consistency about how you felt about yourself in relationship to God at those times? Were you humbled, affirmed, empowered, freed, subdued? How do these actual experiences fit or conflict with the way you normally *think* about relationship with God?

I find that many people's images and concepts of God are very different from their real-life experiences with God. They think they have never experienced a divine presence, but their lives are full of moments of inexplicable love and beauty. They think God is severe or distant, but their direct experience has been of warmth and intimacy. They think they are unworthy of being loved, yet love has come to them in countless simple ways.

It is as if our consciousness resides in two very different worlds: one that is real and one that we think. From our thinking world, we find it difficult to trust the authenticity of our real experience. If you sense a similar discrepancy in your own reflection, don't even try to bring the two together. Insofar as you have the courage to do so, just go for the real, and leave the other stuff behind.

Opening the Vistas

Take it a little further now, and ask the most important question: What do your reflections say about how God might be inviting a more conscious, intentional relationship right now? See if you can differentiate between dry routines and fresh possibilities. Remember to stay involved with God's presence here and now. If you have a sense of that presence, appreciate it and look for guidance from it. You might even save yourself a lot of time by just asking, "What's called for now?" If there is no sense of the holy, it still wouldn't hurt to ask. And sprinkle little interior glances everywhere, and keep coming home to immediacy.

Ask yourself some of the following questions about your sense of God: How and where do I sense God to be when I pray? Does God seem to be far away or close inside? Does God seem more like another person, or more like a cosmic presence? Do I tend to relate to God as parent or creator, as a divine person, as cosmic spirit? What do I expect God's attitude to be toward me? Does God seem more like a judgmental authority, an accepting and loving companion, a dancing lover, an impartial presence? How do my thoughts and concepts about God fit my actual experience? How much is habit? How much seems fresh, immediate, and real?

Similarly, explore your sense of yourself in relationship to God. What kind of attitudes do you normally assume about yourself when you pray? Who is the typical "me" that you bring into prayerful relationship with God? Your feelings about yourself are likely to change dramatically depending on what is going on in your life, but look for any qualities that seem especially common or habitual. Consider whether in relationship to God you tend to sense yourself as being worthwhile or unworthy, childlike or mature, guilty or righteous, weak or competent, courageous or fearful, suspicious or trusting, loving or isolated, open or defensive, and so on. Are such qualities different from how you typically feel about yourself? For example, you might normally sense yourself as a timid and somewhat fearful person, but you might feel very comfortable and at ease in turning to God. Or the opposite might be true: maybe you think of yourself as outgoing but feel a certain shyness in prayer.

If you take a little time with this kind of reflection, I think you will be left with a somewhat clearer sense of the mystery of how you normally relate to God and perhaps of how God has been wanting to relate to you. You may also notice that sometimes your prayerful presence is very natural and spontaneous, while at other times it seems to be contrived or postured. This will be of value as you seek to walk through the moments of your life in more intentional relationship with God. You will be able to let the relationship be more honest, more immediately real, and more freshly God-given.

Hopefully, you may begin to get a sense of something that has been going on between you and God consistently throughout your life, some deep, holy current that has not been influenced by the surface waves and storms of your daily experience. Remember that practicing the presence of love is not really an attempt to bring something new into your life. On the contrary, it seeks only to increase your consciousness of the divine reality that has always been and will always be there for you, in absolute consistency yet rising afresh in every immediate moment. It is not finding something new but uncovering and loving something that has been there all along, something that can *make* everything new.

Images of Relationship

Ideally, our conscious relationship with God should be one in which we can allow ourselves to be who we are, just as we are, and allow God to be who God is, just as God is. It calls for a relinquishment of playacting, a radical willingness to be undefended before the source of love. In this practice more than in any others, we need to ask God to give us a sense and way of relationship instead of rushing into self-created images.

This is not to say that everything should always be radically new or different. There is a place for the tried and true, for habits that are helpful instead of confining, for returning to familiar ways and styles that provide depth instead of escape. As we have seen, there are many old reliable images of relationship with God in spiritual traditions, some of which are almost universal. If one or more of these seem authentically to be given, do not shy away because they are archaic or bring back old unpleasant memories. It may be a very needed thing to recover some of the past in order to be more free in the present. We have covered a number of old images and ways, but let me mention a few more.

Francis de Sales said that people should nurture a sense of walking through life with God like a little child walking along a path with a loving parent. Always holding on to the parent's hand, the child looks at all the sights going by, touches the flowers and berries, and repeatedly looks up into the parent's eyes. Always exploring, appreciating, discovering life, the child never leaves the parent's side.

Teresa of Avila, like so many other Christian pilgrims, tried to imagine Jesus being present beside her or with her wherever she went and whatever she did. Teresa could not picture things in her mind; she had little ability for visual imagery. So she used statues, flowers, water, and other real objects to remind her, and used her intellect to think of Christ being wherever she was as a real physical presence.

Thomas Kelly suggested the practice of going through all one's activities with a continual attention to the divine light "behind the scenes." It was a remembrance of God's presence as a kind of background to everything outside and the center of everything inside, not a person but a very real power and presence.

The possibilities are endless. In my experience, the most valuable images have been ones I would not have chosen objectively for myself. Most have come in surprising ways, and some have been very challenging. As an example, I avoided any images of Jesus for many years. I had had an overdose of such images in Sunday school as a child, and I had many negative associations to them. I much preferred a cosmic, generalized sense of God as love, light, divine presence. But there came a time when very strong, solid images of Jesus kept cropping up. In prayer, I might see him walking toward me. It was the complete Sunday school picture: long hair, flowing white robe, sandals, the works. In meetings with other people, I might sense him there in the room. For a time I even had a picture of his face looking out from inside me, seeing what I was seeing, sending beams of love wherever I looked.

I tried to resist the images. I judged them to be distractions, and to tell the truth they scared me. But I also sensed that they were somehow being given. After a time, I began to accept the images with a little more hospitality. I do not know how or why, but I was somehow empowered to put up with my uninvited visitor. He became less a distraction and more a welcomed guest. I even stopped worrying about what might be image and what might be real. I had not invited this picture-book Jesus, but I had invited God's presence, and if it chose to take that form it was all right with me.

It became better than all right. For quite a while the images of Jesus remained deep and lively vehicles for my ongoing sense of relationship with God. I think they also healed some of the wounds of my early religious training. They freed me of some of my baggage. It has been a long time now since I have had any such sense. Sometimes I miss it. I could bring the pictures back if I wanted—it happens just now thinking of it as I write. But now it is simply another thought I have. It is not given, and it does not have power. Actually, it has been a very long time since I have had any visual images of the divine One. I am aware that I do miss them, but it is all right. Better than all right.

If you feel an authentic desire for images to help realize your ongoing relationship with God, pray for them and watch for them. And don't be too surprised if what is given is not what you expect. It may be that nothing at all seems to be given. If so, try to have the willingness not to create something artificially. As with all the ways of practicing love's presence, it is our authentic desire and willingness that counts, not the specific experience or lack of experience.

Sometimes a truly imageless way is called for. Perhaps all that is needed is a simple, undifferentiated sense, like a consciousness of our desire for God or a delicate feeling of the love of God that surrounds and pervades us all together. Perhaps it is only an attitude that is given: a seeking of divinity in the people we encounter, a turning to the source of love when we think our own thoughts, or a willing vulnerability, stretching and yielding into love in every action we take. Maybe it is only a dim knowing that God is, and it is sufficient.

At other times, we may be called primarily to act out our relationship by means of what we do in our daily lives. Any authentic sense of relationship with God should bear fruit in how we live, but sometimes our actions *are* our way of relationship. When there is little interior experience of God's presence, we may find the real relationship in interacting with others, in service to others, in care and reverence for God's world and God's children, perhaps in letting ourselves be loved *by* God's children.

Here it is important not to confuse the relationship that is given to us with notions about how we think we should feel or act according to moral guidelines or charitable principles. The differentiation may be difficult at times, because the subtle feelings and attitudes that are authentically given, and the actions that spring from them, will be consonant with true morality and justice. They will be loving rather than hateful, creative rather than destructive, compassionate rather than selfish. In fact, the desire to live a truly moral, just, and loving life is in itself a way of practicing relationship with God. But dedication to morality and justice are still only practices. They can be ways of relating to God, or they can be the fruits of relating to God, but they are not God. Just as we can make idols of our images or magic of our prayers, we can make substitute gods of our attitudes and activities.

Although God's presence is everywhere, no activity, enterprise, or thing that we can fix our attention upon is God. No way of remembering, no inner prayer, no image, no feeling, no attitude, no way of behaving, no sense of relationship, no experience is God. In his sketch of the ascent of Mount Carmel, John of the Cross wrote, "Neither this, nor this, nor this . . . Nothing, Nothing, Nothing, Nothing . . . and even on the Mount, Nothing."[16]

Many people have burned out in ministries of service and social action precisely because they have been worshiping their own activity instead of God. In such instances, burnout can be a blessed time that perhaps should not be forestalled. Like the rock bottom for the substance addict, burnout for the action addict is sometimes the only way he or she can come to know the difference between the means and the end, between good deeds and God.

It is the authenticity of how these means come to us and the honesty with which we receive them that make the difference. In a true attempt to be present to God through a sense of relationship, I do not just try to be loving because it is what my religion tells me to do. Instead, I feel a deep desire for that lovingness—for more than I could ever create on my own. I do not look for God because I think it is what I am supposed to do; I do it because I need to, because of a longing that is not of my own creation. And though I often do try to substitute my actions for God because I can control my actions better than I can control love, I keep discovering that no good activity, no right attitude, no set of rules, no good feeling will ever satisfy my real longing for God. And now and then in especially graced moments, a flash of truly unconditional love bursts through me. Agape reigns for an instant.

In that flash, my actions are determined neither by my conscience nor by my desire. They come from pure, simple loving responsiveness to the needs of the situation at hand. They come from a love that is me but is not mine. I do not disappear in such moments, thank God. I am allowed to hang around and appreciate the beauty. I know it is a partial understanding, but sometimes I think the chief purpose of humankind is that there can be someone to say, "Wow!"

10

CONTEMPLATIVE PRESENCE

Let us love the actual world that never wishes to be
annulled, but love it in all its terror, but dare to embrace it
with our spirit's arms—and our hands encounter the hands
that hold it.
MARTIN BUBER

We have looked at Brother Lawrence's first three ways of practicing presence: remembering, heart prayer, and relationship. It is in the fourth way, contemplative presence, that we appreciate reality—the actual world—most directly and accurately. Brother Lawrence called it a pure gaze that finds God everywhere. In this gaze our attention is most all-embracing and all-encompassing. In consecrated contemplative presence, there is no question of whether one is attending to God or to something else. Everything is present at once, not merged together in a unified mush but resplendent in all its diversity. God holds it all, shines in it all, comes to us through it all. And we are alive in it, part of it, at one with it yet still preciously who we are. It does not matter whether we are active or passive; we are absolutely involved.

I have already said most of what I have to say about contemplation. Everything we have discussed has been viewed from a contemplative perspective, and at several points I have asked you to recall your own contemplative moments: those times of simple presence, of just being in love. Let me list the more important points we have already addressed, and elaborate upon a few:

- The contemplative way of love and life embraces the ways of acting, knowing, and feeling (the good, the true, and the beautiful), and it always reveres the mystery of life.

- It has been described as "pure and total presence," "continually renewed immediacy," "the heart embracing the reality that embraces the heart,"

- It is most frequently defined as an open, panoramic, and all-embracing *awareness*, but it is really this all-embracing awareness brought into fullness of living and action, an attitude of the heart and a quality of presence rather than just a state of consciousness.

- Contemplation does imply a certain wakefulness. It may be bright psychological alertness (a quality of seeking) or more gently unfolding willingness (a quality of welcoming). But the heart is awake. Even in sleep it can be so.

- Neurologically, contemplative moments are pauses in the automatic activity of conditioned brain-cell patterns. Psychologically, they are transient suspensions of compulsion. Philosophically they are "naked intuition," the momentary direct perception that happens before we begin to think or react. Spiritually, they are tastes of freedom for love, little encounters with the *YS*, the spaciousness of salvation.

- Like love itself, contemplation comes as a gift, and cannot be autonomously achieved. The practice of contemplation is the practice of opening one's hands to receive the gift.

- We were all natural contemplatives as children. Most of us have lost the naturalness because we have been so strongly conditioned to pay attention to this thing, to concentrate on that thing. We have come to believe that distractions are real external impediments instead of choices we make.

- Contemplation happens to everyone. It happens in moments when we are open, undefended, and immediately present. People who are called contemplatives are simply those who seek the expansion of the moments, who desire to live in that quality of presence more fully and continually.

- Contemplation requires the willingness, honesty, and courageous desire to face into ourselves just as we are and our world just as it is—no distortions, no exclusions, no avoidances, no anesthesia. It means entering our own emptiness, our unrequited longing.

- Contemplation may lead to deep trust and faith, but not to uninterrupted peace of mind. It opens us in love to the suffering and brokenness of the world as much as to its joy and beauty.

- Contemplation never leaves the present moment. It experiences hopes and plans for the future or memories of the past as happening right here and right now.

- Although contemplation is all-encompassing, it also has a direction or an orientation. Think of standing on a mountaintop on a perfectly clear day. You are able to see the entire panorama around you, but at any given time you must still be facing a certain direction. The direction is your choice. Or think of standing in the doorway of your home, your arms open to welcome with hospitality anyone who comes. Still it is your home where you stand, and you have chosen to open your arms to the world.

- We must choose what our direction or orientation will be—what our contemplation is *for.* Contemplative practice brings expanded perception, enhanced responsiveness, and greater self-knowledge. These can be used to destroy as well as to create, for efficiency as well as for love. Our contemplation will serve whatever we dedicate ourselves to.

- Consecrated contemplation is dedicated to God. It faces Godward, opening its arms to the source of love. In consecration, every contemplative moment is being in love; every action arising from our consecration is meant for love.

- Consecrated contemplation, whatever form it takes, is contemplative *prayer,* and it leads to an appreciation of God's need for us as well as our need for God.

There is no way to create contemplative presence; all we can do is nurture our willingness for it. Any attempt to create a contemplative attitude will lead to frustration or, worse, to self-delusion. By definition, willingness for contemplative presence means to stop trying to make anything special happen, to quit making the extra efforts we normally make to determine the kind of experience we are going to have. It involves a giving over of control of our own experience into God's trustworthy hands.

In opening to contemplative presence, we must finally come to clarity about the natural, graced balance and rhythm of stretching and yielding. One might even say that contemplative prayer is nothing other than consecrated naturalness of stretching and yielding. Remember that stretching is not exactly the same thing as tension, and yielding is not quite the same as relaxation. Instead, think of stretching as reaching and opening, and yielding as acceptance and letting-be. Stretching is the self-claiming dimension; yielding is the welcoming dimension. Stretching is like hopeful aspiration; in it the *power* of our selfhood is expressed. Yielding is like hopeful hospitality; in it the *dignity* of our selfhood is expressed.

Do not equate stretching with activity and yielding with passivity. We stretch and yield into action and movement, and we also stretch and yield into rest and repose. In a purely secular sense, our big trouble as human beings is that in trying to master our lives we destroy the natural balances between stretching and yielding. We overstretch to make something happen, or overyield to get what we want. Then we feel uncentered, and try to correct things by going overboard in the opposite direction. It is like trying to set a pendulum or a plumb line. You put it where you think it should be, and discover that it's not quite right. You try to correct it and find you have gone too far the other way. Sooner or later you have to let go and allow it to find its place. Contemplative practice is allowing the plumb line of one's being to find its place. Consecrated contemplative practice—contemplative prayer—is allowing the source of love to bring us toward the place which is our home.

All-inclusiveness

It should be clear by now, but let me say it outright; do not make a distinction between contemplation and action. In the shorthand jargon of spirituality, people often associate contemplation with quiet stillness and action with concerted movement. Thus we have contemplative versus apostolic communities, prayer versus social action, Sabbath versus ministry, and so on. I have even heard some people maintain that extroverts have more trouble with contemplation than introverts. It is just not true. *Everybody* has trouble with contemplation.

We keep making such distinctions and compartmentalizing things in every aspect of our lives—and then we struggle to integrate what we have set apart. We think we must integrate our masculine side with our feminine, our feeling with our thinking, our psychology with our spirituality, our prayer with our active life, our passivity with our assertiveness, our right brain with our left, our body with our spirit, our work with our family, our sexuality with our spirituality. The contemplative option is this: do not make the separations in the first place. If we could just quit drawing so many hard lines between this and that, we could get on with living instead of worrying about integration.

The First Step

Traditional forms of contemplative prayer are usually taught in the context of relaxation. Let your muscles relax, your breathing ease, your mind settle down. Turn it over to God. Just be here, now as you are, in the world as it is, letting God be who God will be. This makes sense for most of us, because most of us are too tense, and relaxing nudges our plumb line in the direction of a little better balance. But now and then we might be too relaxed. Is it possible? We could be dulled, lethargic, bored to death, just wanting to drop out of everything into anesthetized languor. Or we could be naively trusting in everything that comes along, unwilling or unable to even choose a direction in which to face. Then it might make sense to tense up a little bit. Concentrate on a particular thought or image for a while, count your breaths, tighten your muscles, get your act together, and work at it a bit.

Neither relaxation nor tension will bring us to a balance of stretching and yielding, but they may be necessary preliminaries. Sometimes I am so caught up in worries and activities or so dulled by repetition and boredom that I need some help to relax before I can even entertain a hope for naturalness. It does get that bad for me; I assume it does for you as well. It as if the plumb line itself is so tangled and knotted that it can't even hang straight. We need to get the knots out before we can even begin to consider balance. Anything we can do to relax and come into the present moment will help here, but once again the most important thing is to pray. Whether the prayer finds words or is a silent helpless plea, it is the beginning of everything.

Trust and Faith

Contemplative practice begins with a consecrated trust in God that allows us to be just as we are in our situation just as it is. This may seem like a very passive state, in which we are "letting go and letting God" as completely as possible. Indeed, the early stages of a contemplative attitude may be exactly so. But as the attitude deepens, and our stretching-yielding finds its center, we discover that being just as we are includes our desires and judgments, our actions and responses, even our addictions, distractions, and dullness.

This means developing an attitude of real permissiveness with our minds, allowing our thoughts and experiences to happen naturally within God's love, without trying to control them. It means trusting God's grace in ourselves as much as trusting God's grace outside of us. If we are seeking willingness for a God-centered presence that is open to things just as they are, we need to ease our attempts to make anything special happen; we need to try to let our minds and our senses be free. At the outset, we also need to ease our usual attempts to filter or censor our experience; we need to quit trying to keep some things out of awareness while letting other things in. We have to rest the part of ourselves that says, "This thought is a good one; that one is not good," or, "This is what I want to focus on; I don't want to be thinking about that." In other words, we need to be in a position of not labeling anything a distraction. We need to be open to whatever comes to our awareness: thoughts, feelings, images, memories, sounds, sights, and so on. Everything is acknowledged as part of what is happening in the present moment, no matter how important or ordinary, sacred or mundane, good or bad.

It is a very vulnerable place to be, and the very idea of such openness is threatening to many people. It takes only a little experience to know that many things that come to us are not good at all. There are bad things in ourselves and in our world, things we do not want to encourage and things we do not want to be open to. Evil is real, whether we see it as our own ignorance and delusion, as a separate power, or both. There are things we have to say no to, things we must act against; it would be naive and dangerous to assume that everything inside and outside us is good.

The only way we can reconcile real openness with the reality of the world and ourselves is through a committed trust in God. We are not wholly good, and neither is the world around us, *but God is*. And God's grace is not only with us but *in* us. God's grace and love are infinitely strong and absolutely trustworthy. It is only through consciously consecrating ourselves to the immediate presence of God that we can hope to feel safe enough to ease our self-erected defenses.

It goes back to John of the Cross's "nothing." There is nothing in the universe—no thought, no belief, no relationship, no community, no form of prayer, nothing—that is good enough and strong enough for us to trust completely, nothing but God. It is only in trusting God's loving presence that we can find the space and freedom to allow completely natural stretching-yielding. Hence Brother Lawrence's description: pure gazing upon the loving sight of God everywhere.

The trust, which is faith in action, comes to us in many different ways. Faith is a gift, but the degree to which we can trust it, by opening within any given situation, depends upon the choices we make. The question, in any moment, is, Can I trust God here and now? To the extent that we can answer yes, stretching-yielding becomes spontaneous and natural.

I do not have any suggestions about how to deepen faith. It grows as our spiritual life grows, and it comes in surprising and unpredictable ways. The entire notion of practicing loving presence is both an exercise of faith and a response to it. But I can say that trusting is the practice of faith, the stretching-yielding of faith. There is a dimension of learning here, a growth of confidence that comes through repeatedly choosing to trust in God and finding, again and again, that God is trustworthy. But still, in the beginning and in the end, faith is a gift.

From a practical standpoint, trust needs to be very specific and very intentional when we nurture contemplative presence. Any situation can be approached prayerfully if we remember to do so, and the act of easing our autonomous controls can be a very conscious decision to trust God's presence. Whether we feel God's presence or not, we can choose to act in accordance with it. And because God is never absent from us, trusting is always possible—the option is present everywhere, all the time. There is no reason to be worried about the extent or depth of our faith. All we need to do is consciously choose to trust as much as possible in God's loving presence, and in this trust, open.

I must reiterate that trusting God's presence in a given situation is very different from trusting the situation itself. Choosing to open to the situation in the knowledge that God is lovingly present is very different from choosing to open in the belief that the situation itself is trustworthy. The first is mature faith, a consecrated risking-into life as it is; the other is gullibility, naïveté, or superstition.

Of the various ways toward contemplative presence, it seems to me that this sacred trusting is the most direct. One of my colleagues was recently leading a group in contemplative prayer. At various times during the silence, she spoke to the group very quietly: "Is there anything that is not trusting in God?" Those simple words were for me one of the most direct guideposts toward contemplative presence I have known.

Wakefulness

Just as we associate contemplation with relaxation, we also assume it involves wakefulness. In the beginning at least, that is true. In order to be consciously present in love through all things, we need to be awake as well as relaxed. Many people in our society find it very difficult to combine wakefulness with relaxation. We have been conditioned to associate relaxation with drowsiness or sleepiness, and to associate alertness with tension. For this reason, you may find your awareness becoming somewhat dull as you think about relaxation, or you may find yourself tensing up when you think about being wide-awake and present.

Some practice, and not a little grace, is necessary before wakeful relaxation can come. It is worth practicing by itself: can you, just now, relax and wake up at the same time?

If you find it difficult, you may want to try a special exercise with your breathing. As you breathe in, try to sense some vigor and energy, as if you were taking a deep breath of fresh air at an open window early in the morning. Feel yourself waking up, energized, inspired as you inhale. Then, as you exhale, let your breath out with a little sigh, relaxing the muscles of your body, as if you were just finishing some strenuous activity and were ready to rest. It is a little like stretching and yielding, but you have to separate them, move into them sequentially. Repeat this sequence for a while—energy and vigor as you breathe in, sighing and relaxing as you breathe out—and notice how you begin to feel. The rhythm of wakefulness and relaxation with your breathing leads you to a comfortable, easy, but wide-awake kind of presence. This is just the quality you might want to encourage at the beginning.

Later on, as trust and faith deepen and as stretching and yielding come together, entertain the possibility of contemplative presence in dullness or even in sleep. Although there is some wakefulness necessary in any real presence, the most authentic wakefulness is something going on very deeply, well beneath your psychological state of mind. It is the awakening of the heart, in which your soul is saying something to God. You do not and cannot know what is being said—only that it is loving. "I sleep," says the bride, "but my heart is awake."

At this level, the superficial comings and goings of alertness or relaxation seem very relative. They are waves on the face of the ocean, sometimes flowing with the deep, true current, sometimes buffeted by the wind. The waves are attention, rising and falling, moving this way and that, occupied here and there. The deep current is the true life of love. It feels right and good when the waves and current flow together, but it is the current that counts.

Practice

The best practice is that which comes as a gift, the way for this moment that rises from the deep currents into your conscious awareness. If you can be authentically responsive to the grace in this instant, the practice is no practice at all. It is simply the living of your love.

The next best thing is something I have mentioned frequently: consecrate and just be. Even the consecration need not be a formal thing; it can come quite naturally.

The third best thing is also something we have covered: look through your life, identify moments when contemplative presence has come upon you spontaneously, and see if you can recover that quality of being. Then consecrate and just be.

The fourth best thing is something you develop yourself: some consecrated sequence of prayer and centering that helps you come home to the stretching-yielding balance of presence.

The fifth best thing would be a process you find in cooperation with your spiritual friends or community, people who know contemplative prayer and who know you well.

The sixth best thing—or perhaps it is the twelfth—might be something along the following lines:

- Find a good place and settle into a comfortable position. It is worth considering both the place and your body position. Where and what do you think would be most helpful? Inside or outside? Lying down or sitting up? Eyes open or closed? My instructions are meant for sitting still, but if you are a mover you might adapt them to walking.

- Take a little time to identify your desire and consecrate yourself toward the source of love. You might also want to dedicate the time for the sake of someone or something beyond yourself. Either way, ask for God's guidance and help as you seek to be openly present in love. Sometimes I make it a fairly formal prayer. "During this time, God, I want to put myself completely in your hands; I give this time to you, and will try to be present to whatever comes, trusting in your grace."

- Slowly scan over your body, from feet to head or head to feet, noticing how it feels, especially areas that seem extra tense. If it seems natural to let the tension be, by all means do so. If not, stretch a little and shift your position as needed to find more relaxation. Think of your body stretching-yielding into the here and now. Take as much time as you need. You might find that some images help. Sometimes I have a sense of intentionally relaxing into God's loving care, trusting my body into the arms of its creator. Sometimes I even have an image of being like the beloved disciple, leaning back upon the breast of Christ.[1]

- Expand your attention to include your breathing. Don't switch your attention sharply from your body to your breathing, but see if you can let your awareness become larger so it *includes* your breathing. You may want to spend a little time with the wakefulness-relaxation breathing exercise described above, to help you become more alert and to encourage inclusive attention. When you are ready, notice your breathing in the same way that you scanned your body. If you find your breath to be short, rapid, tense, see if it seems right to leave it that way. If not, intentionally let it slow down and become deeper.

- Then ease your control of your breath as much as possible. Relinquish it. In whatever way feels most comfortable, let your breath be natural. Trust it to God. I sometimes find it helpful to entertain an image of letting the Spirit breathe me.

- When your breath becomes more easy and natural, expand your attention once again, toward a full awareness open to everything going on within and around you. Be open to body sensations, breathing, the sights and sounds around you, any thoughts that might surface, any feelings or images that might come to you. Here you may want to think of giving control of your mind and attention into God's care. Sometimes I entertain an image of trusting my mind to the mind of Christ, being willing for God's great consciousness to care for my own.[2]

- Then, insofar and for as long as it is possible, just rest in this simple, open presence. Come back as you need to, perhaps repeating one or more of the above steps. But do not try to hold on to anything, and try neither to make anything extra happen nor to keep anything from happening.

- When it is finished, do not end anything. Acknowledge the moment with honest prayer. It might be thanksgiving, intercession for others, asking for guidance and empowerment as you move into the next present moment. Try to let the prayer happen within the all-inclusiveness of contemplative presence instead of switching from one kind of attentiveness to another. And feather yourself out, the presence of this moment flowing gently into the next, and the next, and the next.

If you go through every step that I have suggested, and do it religiously, you will probably never make it to real contemplative presence. You will spend all your time in preliminaries. But that is all right. The preliminaries, for me, have often been my way of seeking the fullness. They express my desire and point me in the direction. Beyond that, nothing but God's grace matters. Any other consideration will turn the whole thing into a project. Besides, spending time in preliminaries helps us know another meaning of practice. Practicing means "not yet fully accomplished." Could it be any other way in the spiritual life? In practicing contemplation, we are practicing to become contemplative. In practicing being in love, we are practicing becoming love.

During the Rest of the Day

As with Brother Lawrence's three other ways, experience with very open, immediate presence during set-aside prayer expands naturally into savoring the same quality of presence at various times during the rest of the day. Sometimes it happens spontaneously, and you simply notice and appreciate it more than before. At other times, you will want to remember it and make a conscious choice to be willing for it to happen. You may be able to "just be present," or you might need to move through the above sequence in a very abbreviated way. With a little practice, you can move through the body-breath-mind steps within the space of a few seconds. Even better, it all condenses into one consecrated stretching-yielding.

You may find it helpful to go through something like this as you enter into situations, especially those in which you are most likely to be kidnapped and forgetful. But beware of turning it into a psychological method. You may well find that you feel better and function better when you cultivate a contemplative attitude, but I caution you not to "use" it to cope with stressful situations or to increase your efficiency. Try to remember your original desire and intent and the hazards of chasing after an artificial state.

There are many distortions that can creep into contemplative practice; as I have indicated, there are plenty of ways to do it wrong and no way to do it right. The very idea of "doing it" in the first place gets us into trouble. For this reason, a little extra reflection and review of contemplative practice may be helpful.

If you have established a way of daily reflection, this additional review can be made a part of it very easily. One way or another, I encourage you to consider the following questions prayerfully:

1. In seeking open, willing presence, have I been adding anything extra to my presence? Am I holding on to anything extra, censoring anything, grasping at anything, trying to control anything more?

2. Have I found myself stifling or stopping my mind or heart in any way, rather than being free in God's care?

3. Has my awareness felt dulled, dazed, or trancelike rather than simply open and present? If I have established a routine, is it really helping, or am I escaping into it?

4. Is there any way that I have been working at it, putting extra effort into it, trying to make something happen or keep something from happening rather than letting things be natural and spontaneous?

5. Does the practice seem to be having any effect on my relationships with other people? If so, does it seem that I am more or less lovingly present?

Be especially careful about the fifth question; it is perhaps the most important and surely the most tricky. By now you should be clear that "loving presence" with other people is not something you can measure by the number of good deeds done or your own or other's expectations met. In some cases love is tough, and it will make people unhappy. In other cases, your own response to love may involve a temporary pulling-back from some relationships, and it may take some time before you can return in greater fullness. So do not jump to hasty conclusions. It will also be helpful if you can go over your reflections with someone who has a better perspective on your situation.

Increasing Simplicity

If you find that you are missing the mark in one way or another with your practice, you are probably trying too hard or complicating it too much. The body-breath-awareness practice I have described is filled with considerable doings and possibilities for making things happen. In real contemplative presence, all these things are extra. Like any other methods, they are things to do that we hope will lead toward a more contemplative attitude. And like other methods, they inherently complicate the essence of real presence.

I know I am repeating myself, but all methods of practice, all ways and means exist only because we are so addicted to having to always be doing something. The doings are needed only to the extent that our minds become desperate without them. They are helpful only insofar as they usher our minds through the withdrawal symptoms that accompany simplification. If we hold on to any method of prayer or meditation beyond this point, we may be making an idol of it; we need to consider whether we have given ourselves to the method instead of to God. I emphasize this so much because I have done it so much. Time and again I have found something I can do to help me pray, and then later discover I am doing that thing instead of really praying. It is more comfortable to cling to a spiritual doing than to really give myself to the precariousness of prayer, to the loving but unknown mystery of God.

So simplify whenever and wherever you can. Drop whatever doings you can do without. Move backward through my list of "next best things" as far as you can. Explore the edges of being without methods to prop you up, where you must trust God instead of your own knowledge or abilities.

Active Contemplation

If you are indeed letting yourself be who you are before God, then the "you" you are letting be includes everything in you that is true and natural. It includes your knowledge, your experience, your capacity to judge and to choose, your common sense, your responsiveness, and your ability to act. Nothing is excluded! Letting your body be, for example, means letting it move when it becomes uncomfortable, letting it respond to the situations in which it finds itself. To let your mind be means to let it make the judgments and discriminations that it will naturally. If you do indeed let your mind be in the light and love of God, then you will very naturally appraise situations and respond to them. You will neither suppress your own natural activities—because that would be extra—nor simply follow every impulse that comes your way, because that would necessitate the suppression of your discrimination and judgment. All your faculties, all your abilities are available. But because of your consecration, nothing happens outside of or apart from your concern for love.

This means that contemplative presence is often very active indeed. Work needs to be done; people need attention; things that are wrong need to be put right; justice needs to be served; joy and play and humor need to be expressed. Most of all, love needs to be fulfilled. All this must be able to happen within contemplative presence, in God, with God. *True contemplative presence is the realization (making real) of living, moving, and having our very being in God.*

If this description has begun to make your head spin, do not feel alone. It is impossible to fully comprehend this quality of presence. From the outside, a person with a truly contemplative heart may appear no different from anyone else. But inside, the difference is radical. Nothing happens apart from God's presence. And when the situation calls for it, the person's responses may then be seen for what they are: willing to sacrifice life itself in the cause of love.

Negative and Positive Ways

In my own experience—which has by no means approached the purity of willingness I have just described—I find it very difficult to approach contemplative presence in a positive way. I cannot select an image of what the presence is like and then seek it. For me, the way is more negative; I do best by simply stopping what is clearly not part of this presence. When I feel I must handle something on my own, autonomously and without reference to God, I know it is time for something to ease up. When I find myself creating something artificial, when I feel the all-too-familiar sense of desperation, clinging, grasping beyond a willingness for God, I know it is time to pray. The negative way, then, is one that simply looks for mistakes and errors, and trusts that God will take care of the truth. This is why my friend's words meant so much to me: "Is there anything that is not trusting in God?"

Because mine seems to be the negative way, I am somewhat at a disadvantage in describing a positive way. There are two examples from Christianity that occur to me. The first is to consider what we know through scripture of Jesus as a person. Throughout history, many great spiritual seekers have sought to live life as Jesus lived it, to model every intention after the image of the carpenter's child from Nazareth. Part of the imitation of Christ involves attempting to follow Jesus' teachings and commandments as they apply to one's external activities. This requires considerable emphasis on doings, especially in the realms of prayer, service, justice, and compassion.

But a true seeking of Jesus must also include an attempt to get into his heart and mind, a seeking of his interior experience. This leads—I think inevitably—to the realization that Jesus was never consciously apart from his "abba," his God. Certainly he had times of prayer in solitude, but there is no indication that during the rest of his days he was on his own. All the evidence points in the opposite direction: that he was in continual communion, even union, with God, and that this oneness with God in no way disrupted or minimized the fullness of his humanity. Even in those ancient words of despair from the cross, "My God, my God, why have you forsaken me?" he expressed his constant givenness to God. To seek to imitate this interior experience, then, is to nurture the true meaning of incarnation; whether or not the presence of God is experienced, nothing, *nothing* need happen apart from God. Or to put it more positively, every-thing, *everything* can happen within the consciousness of God's presence.

Another positive image of contemplative presence is the story of Jesus with Mary and Martha. Jesus is invited into the house of these dear friends, and Martha is busy preparing dinner while Mary sits with Jesus. Martha complains that Mary is not helping her, and Jesus tells her that she worries about too many things; only one thing is really necessary, and Mary has chosen it. This is not an easy passage for many people, especially for many women, because on the surface it sounds as though Jesus is criti-cizing Martha for doing the work of preparing the meal and commending Mary for passive listening. But look closely; he is challenging Martha's worries, not her work, and commending Mary's presence, not her docility.[3]

The Greek word used to describe Martha's state of mind is *merimnao*. It means preoccupied to the point of distraction by many things, and comes from the root *merismos,* meaning being pulled asunder. The problem is not that Martha is working, but that she is obsessed with working. Indeed it is Mary who has the contemplative heart; she has chosen the one thing necessary, which is to attend to God. It just happens that in this particular moment she does it by sitting still; in another time, perhaps even in the next moment, she could do the same thing *while* helping with the work. The story might have been better told that way. It might have been better still if Jesus had been helping with the work. But Martha's problem was that her preoccupation had kidnapped her awareness away from the divine presence.

Many people in this day and time would like to draw a line between their actions and their prayer. They might even go so far as to say, "God gave me a will, so God wants me to act on my own." But there is no scriptural justification for this, and neither is there any need. Surely God gives us the freedom to act with or without conscious attention to the source of love. But what God *wants*, and what our hearts most deeply seek, is for us to live every moment, do every act, breathe every breath in conscious immediacy with the One who is all love.

11

LOVING IN THE WORLD

Like billowing clouds, like the incessant gurgle of the
brook, the longing of the soul can never be stilled. It is
this longing with which holy persons seek their work
from God.

HILDEGARD OF BINGEN

It is not an easy thing to be mindful of love in the world. It can
happen only when our longing catches us like hunger pangs, or
when we are given the grace of real presence in the midst of
things. We can remind ourselves as much as possible, and pray
for God to remind us of love throughout the day, but it is only
grace that makes it happen. We find ourselves in many different
contexts and roles as we move through our days. In one way or
another, all of us are involved in homemaking, finance, politics,
education, art, religion, human relationships, justice, science,
ecology, and a host of other concerns. In all these settings we
may find support and nurturance for loving presence. In all of
them we will also encounter resistance and sabotage. I want to
address just the contexts of work and home as examples. The
insights we can find there apply everywhere.

In the Workplace

Ideally, our work is cocreation. It is the exercise of our bodies
and minds stretching-yielding into birthing and nurturing the

world. Ideally, work is consecrated. It is something that happens within the present moment, like the old Zen image of chopping wood and carrying water. When you chop wood, you chop wood. When you carry water, you just carry water. It is nothing separate from the ongoing play of love. Ideally, work is just another beautiful form of joining the cosmic sparkle. But this is an ideal. You may approach it if you are an artist or if you work with plants, animals, and the earth. I have been given the precious gift of approaching the ideal in my work of spiritual guidance, teaching, and writing. But your work may seem quite far from the ideal. Mine was not always so satisfying.

I worked as a psychiatrist in public institutions (military and state hospitals and prisons) for nearly twenty years. During the last twelve of those years, I was consciously trying to be mindful of love, to practice the presence of God. It was the most frustrating thing I ever tried to do. I was very diligent; I prayed and meditated in the morning, and I reminded myself while driving to work. I could be conscious, consecrated, and grounded in the present moment all the way there, but as soon as I entered the ward everything changed. I was immediately kidnapped. I was gone: away from the present, away from any sense of love or its source, away from even appreciating my own being. It was not a gradual transition; it felt like a thief in the night stealing my soul. One moment I was there; the next I was gone.

Where did I go? I didn't even know at the time. Looking back, it seems clear that I went into my sense of responsibility for the diagnosis and care of the patients. There were usually too many patients and too few staff; care was rudimentary at best, and it took all my efforts just to try to keep from prescribing the wrong medication or releasing a dangerous person. And there was so much paperwork! The stresses on the staff were incredible. But I did take breaks; I drank coffee and ate lunch and talked and joked with people. There would have been time and space for a little remembrance, but I kept forgetting. I even had time to teach a little meditation practice to patients and staff—and even during that teaching I forgot! I think it helped some of the people there, but it surely did nothing for me.

Most days I would remain forgetful until my work was done and I was driving home. Then I would remember, and such sadness would fill me. Where had I been? How could I have allowed myself to be so captured? I can remember driving home one day after I had spent a long time feeling helpless with a very disturbed patient. I actually slapped myself in the face when I realized I could have been praying for her and praying for myself instead of just worrying about what to do. I tried everything. I put notes on my desk and ignored them. I put pebbles in my shoes and got used to them. I scheduled spaces for quiet in the middle of the day, only to fill them up with paperwork.

Nor was I alone in the struggle. Since the early 1970s I had been working part-time with the Shalem Institute for Spiritual Formation, leading groups and giving workshops. The community of Shalem's staff was as supportive, as challenging, and as prayerfully helpful as anyone could hope for in a gathering of pilgrims. I discussed my struggles with them and with my spiritual director. I had people praying for me, friends and family supporting me. All the right things were in place—more right things than most people have the advantage of—and still it did not "work."

It was a long time of spiritual suffering. It was not a dark night in the true sense; other things in my life were going along well, and I frequently had a strong sense of God's presence in places other than at work. But my spiritual failure to be present in love at work seemed like a huge, painful abyss, a gaping wound cut into the middle of every day. Nothing helped; nothing made it better. I couldn't understand it. And it went on for twelve years.

It stopped only when I left the psychiatric institutions and started working full-time with Shalem. For the first few months I felt as though I were in a different world. The caring, supportive atmosphere of the Shalem workplace allowed me to reflect with a bit of perspective on my past work. I began to see some things I had not noticed before. I first became aware of a habit I had developed in the psychiatric work. When I got up every morning, I would put on a kind of psychological armor before going to work. I knew that every day people would be screaming at me, threatening me, making urgent demands. I knew that each day I would be afraid—not so much of being hurt but of making a mistake that might ruin or destroy someone's life. I could not enter that kind of day undefended, and so I established a kind of feeling-barrier against the stresses I would meet.

I suppose most physicians have such a barrier, as do most teachers, law enforcement officers, and lots of other people who have to work in an atmosphere of crisis and hostility. The armor I put on was not much in evidence to others, and it was completely unconscious on my part. Most people thought of me as a caring and humane physician, and I certainly prided myself on being compassionate. I did not know how defended I was until I started working at Shalem. Then, although I kept putting on my armor every day, there was nothing to defend against. No one was threatening me, and the mistakes I made were not going to destroy people's lives. It was the weirdest feeling, defending myself against nothing. I think it took more than a year for the habit of armoring myself to stop. Perhaps it still continues a little—I would be the last one to know. I do know it comes back from time to time. I also know that it is very difficult to practice loving presence with armor on. In my case, for more than a decade, it was impossible.

I have but one response to this insight: compassion. I feel the compassion of forgiveness for my own struggles and failures. I could not help it, and I sure did try. But even more, I feel a great, sad compassion, which at times is almost overwhelming, for the people I left behind in those institutions: the people incarcerated there who must spend twenty-four hours a day defended and the people who still put on their armor every day to work there. Many of them, the nurse's aides and technicians especially, do not have the choice of getting another job. It is a matter of working there or not working at all. They have families and children just as I do, but they are stuck and I was not. I made enough money to help get my kids through school and then could choose to move on. They don't have that kind of freedom. It just isn't fair. Sometimes I even feel guilty about what I taught them of the spiritual life of love. Did I contribute to making some of them feel as bad as I did during those twelve years?

But if we are not to entertain a vision of a loving life, even if it makes us ache in desperation, what hope will there ever be of a better world? The problem in my workplace was not only in me but also in the workplace itself. The institutions that house our dysfunctional people are just downright wrong. I do not know how to make the institutions better, but I do know they are going to have to change. And they are not going to change as long as we adjust to them. It is only with human pain that freedom and dignity come forth.

I go into this detail because what I am saying does not apply only to psychiatric institutions. It applies, to some extent, to almost every institution we have. It applies to education and social work, to government and business, and to religious institutions as well. People are stuck in all these places, and they can neither get out of them nor find a loving quality of presence within them. Love demands defenselessness, and in many if not most of our workplaces that is just too high a price.

But there is more. In reflecting back on my hospital and prison work, I noticed two other things that might have made a difference if I had been aware of them at the time. Both have to do with receiving a gift. First, as you may have detected from my description of my struggles, I had very much made a project of practicing the presence of love. I was trying to do it myself. Sure, I knew enough to ask God for it, but at the time even that was a method: something that should "work" if I did it right. In fact I was trying to engineer my own loving presence. I was not open to its being given. Of course I felt like a failure, and if I had experienced more immediate presence I probably would have considered it a success. For that reason alone, I am now truly grateful that it didn't happen. What I do wish is that I could have understood the difference between receiving a gift and making something happen. Yet it is understandable; you can't be too open when you are covered with armor.

The second observation is like the first. I thought back over those years and collected all the experiences I could recall of little moments of graced presence on the hospital and prison wards. There were only four of them that I could identify in all that time. I'm sure there must have been more, but the memory is as unavailable now as the awareness of love was then. The moments I do recall have a special commonality; all of them happened when I allowed someone else to care for me. I mentioned two of these times in the first chapter: the schizophrenic woman who got a light for my pipe and the serial killer who helped me through a difficult interview. The third was when a patient offered to loan me a quarter for a phone call. The fourth was when the nursing staff helped me clean up my office. I am sad that there were so few such times; there could have been so many more. But I was so caught up in being the helper, the caretaker, the responsible deliverer of health services that it hardly ever occurred to me that I could be cared for as well. It feels so stupid to think I really felt that way, but it is true. I let people care for me at home and at Shalem, and in both those places I felt my own presence for love frequently. But not in the wards. There I was too defended, too responsible, too much needing to stay on top of things, in control.

So if you feel stuck in a situation where practicing the presence seems simply impossible, I would suggest four things. First, consider your receptivity. There are people who would love to affirm you or offer you something, if you could only ask or even just be open to receiving it. And God, perhaps, is also waiting with a gift. I keep thinking of Saint Augustine's old comment that God is always wanting to give us good things, but our hands are always filled with something else. Second, if you feel like a failure at practicing the presence, quit trying to "do" it. Don't just remember that it is a gift, *live* it as a gift. Of course, you could be the opposite of me. Maybe you never do anything for yourself and are always expecting others to give you everything. But somehow I doubt it.

Third, take a look at your armor. It will not be the same color or shape as mine, but I bet you have it. The question is, Do you need as much as you have? Can you risk being a little less defended, a little more vulnerable to what you meet every day? I am not proposing that you can or should try to move into every situation in an absolutely undefended way. It is a matter of not adding anything extra. Examine the threats you face in your work and life. How many of them are real, how many imagined? How many are threats to your person, and how many are just threats to your self-image? What is the worst thing that can happen? It is not easy, but can you perhaps have a little more courage, a little more dignity, and a little more trust in God and your own essential goodness? Sometimes, facing squarely into what threatens you brings even deeper empowerment toward integrity.

The fourth suggestion may be the most difficult. If you find yourself stuck in a workplace or life situation that is truly antagonistic to loving presence, you must ask yourself if you are really as stuck there as you think you are. It may be there truly are no other options, but usually there are; you just don't like them. Be very honest about this; why do you stay where you cannot be open to love? I know why I stayed where I did. It wasn't because of altruism but because I felt I needed a steady income to support my family—in the manner to which we had all become accustomed. The institutions gave me health insurance and a regular paycheck that undergirded the ups and downs of my private practice income. That was it, clear and simple. Your reasons may be quite different, but the question is, Are they necessary? Perhaps you remain out of loyalty, or because you don't want to be a quitter, or because like Hamlet you would rather bear the ills you have than fly to others that you know not of. Try to face it honestly.

If you realize that you could indeed leave a love-killing situation, then you need to move into truly prayerful vocational discernment. Perhaps you are being invited to tough it out and discover a way through; maybe there is a possibility of openness to love there that you just haven't been able to find yet. Maybe what's called for is a kind of revolution within the situation; perhaps you can change the structure of things and help create a better atmosphere for love. It even might be possible that you are being invited to suffer and pray there, as an act of intercession for the others who are trapped.

Or maybe it really is time to get out. Some institutions just

need to wither away from their own gangrene, and your leaving
may mercifully hasten the end. As I have said before, we cannot
know such things with absolute certainty, but with enough
prayer, consultation, and honest reflection we are given a sufficient basis for decision making. Before we even begin, however,
we must have the guts to face our situation honestly and directly.
We often think of needing courage to do what must be done,
but I think the real courage comes in making a truly prayerful,
discerning decision in the first place.

The first prayer of all, then, might be for courage. But understand that gracious courage is not the kind of intestinal fortitude
we usually think of. It is not a matter of steeling yourself, tensing
your muscles, girding your loins, or any other kind of armoring.
It is not a building up of autonomous power, but a refuge in the
power of love. Like all other graceful hopes, it is opening to a
gift. Echoing the psalmists, Hildegard prays, "This supreme longing pulls me to you, beckons me to come under your protection,
into the shadow of your power."[1]

In the Home

By home, I mean to refer to the closest, most committed and
abiding human relationships we have. These include close
friendship, community, marriage, and family. I have a friend who
says marriage and family are the great functional asceticisms of
life. If they can't grind down your pride and strip off your addictions, nothing will. It's true, and it applies to all the relationships
that constitute our home. God willing, it is also a good deal of
fun. The fun part is the roller coaster of relationship. Who is
doing what to whom and why? Many people think of the ideal
family or friendship relationship as being solid, stable, reliable,
one in which you can count on everything staying the same. I

don't know because I've never experienced family quite that way, but it sounds a little boring. The ascetical part is that your family and closest friends pretty much know who you are. You can't get away with as much there.

A few years ago I was away for a week giving lectures and workshops. When I returned home, Betty and the kids welcomed me warmly as they always do. The evening was pleasant, catching up with one another, but I felt just a little strange. I could not put my finger on it, but something seemed not quite right. It wasn't until the following evening that I figured it out. No one here was looking at me as a great authority; not a single person had asked for my wisdom about anything for a whole twenty-four hours! And I was missing it. Thank God that just being at home made me aware of what an ego trip I had begun. I have many ego trips, but not as many as I surely would have if my wife and children and dear friends stopped reminding me that I am just regular old Jerry. My children are adults now, and they tackle the job with glee. My sons and their friends like to call me the Mystickle Theologikan. Pompous images come off in family and abiding friendships, and the defenses either come down gently on their own or get worn down by attrition. That is why I like the ups and downs of family life best.

The other side of family dynamics is stability and security, the homeostasis of the family system, and although I know it is necessary I am more suspicious of it. Like all abiding groups of people, families form habit patterns. When the patterns are efficient or pleasant, we call them family traditions. When the patterns do not work so well, we call them dysfunctional. Either way, too much habit causes us to take one another for granted. It happens in the workplace as well. We become so accustomed to the steady stream of self-sacrifices others make for us that we fail to appreciate their love. It is wonderful to expect and rely upon the abiding support of others in homemaking and other work. It is not at all wonderful to become so habituated that we take that support and the love that continually births it for granted.

The real problem with habit patterns, in families and other institutions as well, is that the most ingrained habits are addictions. Tradition or dysfunction, daily routine or entrenched expectation, our most frozen habits fill up our spaces and limit our freedom for love. Just as love and grace can be astronomically expanded in community, the addictions of families and institutions can be more treacherous, more insidious, and more malignant than anything an individual mind might dream up. And the addictions are more deeply entrenched. Prevent the pattern and the whole group goes into withdrawal symptoms. Let one person seek freedom, and the whole system can collude to undermine it. And nearly always it all goes on unconsciously.

I have never understood all the theory about codependence and dysfunctionality in families, but the theory clearly has its finger on something real. Families, like institutions, do become addicted to destructive patterns of behavior and relationship. Collectively, we become addicted more powerfully, deeply, and rapidly than we do as individuals. And if we cannot free ourselves from our individual addictions without intervening grace, we certainly cannot liberate our families and institutions by the power of will alone.

The terms are not important. Whether you call it dependence or codependence, compulsive collusion or being a slave of love, it happens when love loses its freedom to addiction. It happens in individual psychological attachments, in love between couples, in the habits of family systems, and in every group that seeks security in togetherness. As I have said, you can tell it by its lack of space. You know it when you feel you have no choice and when your dignity as a person comes from something or someone other than the source of love.

If you wake up inside a relationship and find that what you thought was home is really more of a prison, there will be things you must do, courageous things, to reclaim your freedom. And you will need God's grace to empower you. But let us not be too afraid of a little addiction in relationships. If we were to permit ourselves only relationships perfectly free of addiction, we would have no relationships at all. It is impossible. I have said it many times; when you really love someone or something, some addiction is bound to be there. It is all right. Just as our hearts are not meant to have their longings completely fulfilled, we are not meant to live completely without addiction. Once again, you need to choose whether to move toward love's invitation or away from fear's threat. Choose between seeking the light or avoiding the dark. It does not mean addictions are good; they are not. But get out of your either-or mind. Ease your perfectionism and bend a little with the reality of things.

As systems, families and close friendships are powerful forces for both addiction and freedom. Whatever an individual can do, a group can do more emphatically—for good or for ill. Ideally, marriage, family, and friendship could express the best of spiritual community: committed people who know one another very well, who love one another deeply, and who support and pray for one another's awakening of love. In real life, however, all such relationships both support and undermine true love, both encourage freedom and tighten the bonds of attachment. That is the way it is for us as individuals; it can and should be no different in community.

It is also to be expected that we will not really understand one another. Along with fantasies of eternal romance, many people entertain the belief that spouses and others in committed relationships should not only understand each other's spiritual hearts but also share each other's experiences and ways of practice. If that is true, few relationships meet the standard. In talking with hundreds of people about their spiritual life in marriage and community, I know of none who have found complete sharing of spiritual hearts. And only a handful feel fully understood. In all loving relationships there is a blending of understanding and confusion, of support and resistance. It may sound as though there is something wrong with our relationships because of this, but I think it is something right.

Just as we are not meant to have all our yearnings satisfied and our spaces filled as individuals, I think we are also not meant to find perfection in human relationships. I certainly hope this is so, because human relationships can never be perfect. Because our love is always mixed with attachment, any deepening of love's freedom—which means a lightening of attachment—in one partner is bound to cause a certain threat to the attachments of the other. It can help a lot if both parties understand and accept this as inevitable and right, but it is not easy. It can help even more if each party reverences the other's consecration—however different—and both trust God's mercy in the relationship. Then each can celebrate the other's growing freedom. But even then there will be wrenchings of the relationship's foundation. It cannot be avoided, for love calls us to trust more in God than in any relationship. It is all right.

Personal Practice

We must accept our lack of perfection and admit to a certain addictedness in work, at home, and in every other context where we are at all alive and involved. We need to know the all-rightness of it. But that does not mean we need to adjust to it or find peace of mind with it. What is really all right is our willing acknowledgment of the way things are, combined with our passionate desire to make them better. See what is, don't waste time in recriminations, and do your darnedest to nurture love. This is the essence of real-world practice.

Prayer comes at the beginning, in the middle, and at the end of practice—if practice ever really ends. It is prayer of petition, for our own courage, remembrance, and simple presence at work and at home. It is prayer of intercession, for the people at work and at home, that grace might flow through them, free them, and heal their brokenness. It is intercession as well for the systems and institutions that make up our homes and workplaces, prayer for liberation and love in the environments and atmospheres within which people work and pray and long for something better. It is prayer of praise and adoration and thanksgiving, expressing our gratitude for the grace we have been given and our ever-deepening need for more. It is also prayer for guidance: How can I respond, right here and now? What is the real invitation of love in this particular situation? Further, it is prayer for strength, courage, and protection so that we can not only take refuge but also act forthrightly in the shadow of God's wings.[2]

With prayer throughout, as I have said, we can hopefully (literally, being filled with hope) cultivate the openness and simplicity that will allow us to receive the gift of immediate loving presence. Do *not* try to make it happen. Use all the reminders, all the sacramentals and gimmicks that you think might help. Pull out all the stops. Go for it, and let the chips fall where they may. But do not try to make it happen.

Attend to the log in your own eye instead of the specks in the eyes of your family, friends, and coworkers. Seek compassion for how they are stuck, even though it may weigh heavily on you. Notice and appreciate the sacrifices they make and the gifts they have given. But do not betray your dignity. Claim the space and freedom that is your birthright. You may have to make demands for enough space in relationships or breaks in work to reclaim your true desire. You can do it without being nasty. People may not like it, and often they won't understand, but with grace it is possible to be strong without being mean. With grace, all things are possible.

Think of your true home in God's love. It is where your heart is. It is your spiritual home, always right here and right now no matter where you are or what you are doing. Home at home. Home at work. Home anywhere, but always fresh in continually renewed immediacy. Keep coming home, keep returning. And when you are there (here), stretch and yield lovingly into the real-life activity of now.

Try a little consecrated Zen. Do one thing at a time, with complete, immediate mindfulness. Don't do it to get it done so you can get on to the next thing. Do it for love. Do it fully, sensitively, openly. Do it now. *Then* do the next thing. Chop wood. Carry water. Type letters. Read mail. Talk to your friend. Bathe the children. Giggle. Fix dinner. Balance the checkbook. Make love. Drink cocoa. Answer the phone. Complain to your boss. Fix the drainpipe. Walk from here to here. Schedule next month's appointment now. Work on the budget. Hammer the nail. Disagree with your colleague. Change the light bulb.

Life *can* be lived this way. I know it, because I live this way (maybe four or five minutes of every day). The Vietnamese Zen master Thich Nhat Hanh put it this way: "While washing the dishes, you might be thinking about the tea afterwards, and so try to get them out of the way as quickly as possible in order to sit and drink tea. But that means that you are incapable of living during the time you are washing the dishes."[3]

Look for the small, simple places at home and work where living, loving presence happens naturally: in the garden, perhaps, or looking into a child's eyes, or in moments at work when you are really right there. What can those little moments teach you? How can they be nurtured? What brokenness or overloads or excessive attachments stifle the moments and fill up the spaces? What kind of healing is needed? What sort of prayer is called for?

Institutional Practice

Wouldn't it be nice if people at work and home could join together in seeking direct presence for love? It may be more possible than you think. In many workplaces and nearly all homes there is at least some chance for collaboration, some potential for spiritual community. The trouble is, you have to be pretty courageous to seek it out and cultivate it. You have to express something of your heart's desire to the people around you, and that almost always feels very risky.

The first problem is finding words to express your desire. None of them work well. Then, if you are given the grace to stumble into some coherence, what will the response be? Maybe the people around you won't understand at all. Worse, they may understand and feel threatened or disagree. Worse still, they may scorn you. When you are scorned in the expression of your heart's desire, it is your very soul that feels attacked. It is your most tender part, your most vulnerable place. There is no way to justify yourself or to explain it; the more you try, the more awful it feels. Nothing that is authentically spiritual can finally be justified to someone who disagrees.

Sometimes it is better to keep your mouth shut. That is especially true if you find yourself beginning to argue or become defensive. But there are other times when self-revelation is really called for. You never know what people's responses are going to be until you take the risk, and if you never take the risk you will miss many opportunities for spiritual friendship and support. Pray for guidance and courage. Keep your eyes open for clues about the readiness of other people to hear what you might be trying to say. And when you do express yourself, try to do it from your own groundedness in love. Don't lose your foundation, as I have so many times, by talking *about* your desire. Instead, speak *from* it. And be willing to be hurt. Who knows; your home or workplace might become a real resource for communal spiritual deepening. God only knows whether it is possible, but it certainly would be wonderful. It is worth the risk.

I wonder what might have happened if I had taken more risks, let down more of my armor in the psychiatric institutions where I used to work. But it is a moot point; that was a long time ago for me. My present workplace at Shalem is an incredibly rich spiritual community. I have not had to take great risks to help it become that way, because the people around me all take risks. Thus all our risks are a little smaller. They may disagree with me, but I trust them to respect my heart; they will not scorn it. We talk together about our spiritual lives, we pray together, we know we share a common desire, and we are bonded in a common resistance against letting efficiency usurp love. Of course, it is of no small value that the purpose of our institution and the goal of our work is to help people pray. There are a number of other such workplaces around the world, where people have agreed to serve love first, to seek God first, and struggle together to make it possible. How I wish there were more!

Shalem is a very privileged workplace, but it still is not easy. We are flooded with work and constantly tempted toward preoccupation with getting things done. We do conspire together to worship efficiency from time to time. But at least we see it, and we see it together. People like to just drop into our office because it feels so spacious and open compared to their own workplaces in the nation's capital. But it is a matter of perspec-

tive; it usually does not feel so spacious and open to us. I saw
Tilden Edwards, our executive director, running from one office
to another, his arms filled with books and papers, late for another
meeting. He noticed me grinning at him and responded,
"Sabbath is so hard for those of us who talk about it."

We do see it, and we do what we can to make it better. Here
are a few things we have done:

- At our meetings (board of directors, committees, program
  and budget planning, office staff, and so on) we not only
  begin with silent prayer but talk together about what
  prayerfulness and presence means to each of us at the time.
  Often for board meetings, a discussion of prayerfulness is
  the first and last agenda item. We have found it especially
  helpful to discuss it at the end of meetings. Where were we
  most present? Where were we most captured?

- We prayerfully decide together what to do to help make
  things more present and open to love. Over the years we
  have come up with a multitude of gimmicks, including
  ringing bells right in the middle of things, pausing for
  silence between agenda items, rotating people in silent
  prayer throughout the meeting, encouraging individuals to
  call for silence any time they feel pulled away from home.
  Occasionally there is even more silence than there are
  words—but the work gets done.

- In meeting rooms and offices we keep a number of visual
  reminders: candles, icons, flowers, and symbols.

- We play together and share much good humor. We do this
  a lot. Over the years, I think most of us have stopped feeling guilty when someone comes in and finds us goofing off.

- We have regular times of retreat and prayer together, and

we support each individual's having time and space for herself or himself.

There is nothing magical about what we do, and we are a long way from perfection as a loving institution. The most important thing we do is probably just to talk about it with one another. If we come up with a helpful method, we usually find we must change or drop it before long because it becomes routinized. We adapt to it, and it loses its value as fresh. But it is in talking about it that our shared desire and intention come to light. Then to some extent we become consecrated together, and all our methods become empowered. Without a touch of that communal consecration, any method, no matter how creative, would only be an empty routine.

The gift—and we are all aware of its being a gift—is that somehow the grace of God has stayed with us in our struggles to be lovingly present together. Grace has helped us avoid too much competitiveness, too much emphasis on institutional survival, too much self-importance, too much attachment to routine. We pray for that grace to continue for as long as we are meant to be together.

I see the grace happening most vividly in the individual people who make up the community. It is true for every spiritual community. There is always someone who very quietly and prayerfully supports the others. There is always someone to lighten things up when we become too serious and someone to call us back when we have flown too far afield. At any given time, someone is concerned with getting the job done, and someone else is saying it's only loving God that's important.

There is also always someone in a prophetic role, challenging the way we are and demanding something better. Even in this privileged environment, the prophetic role takes courage and requires suffering. Like every system and institution, we become addicted to the ways we do things; we do not want to let them go. It is not easy to be the one who must call for institutional change from the authenticity of his or her own heart. The Christian phrase is "bearing the cross." The military equivalent is "taking the point." Whatever you call it, it is one person leading the rest of us where we do not wish to go.

I do not suggest that you use Shalem's experience as a model for your own work or family setting, any more than you should use my individual experience as a guide to your own. You are unique, and so are your home and your work situation. Maybe there is an idea or an attitude that you can apply to your setting. More important, though, is that you take hope in God's grace as being able to open the way for you, for your home, for your work, and for your world.

12

LOVING FOR THE WORLD

For I tell you this; one loving blind desire for God alone is
more valuable in itself, more pleasing to God and to the
saints, more beneficial to your own growth, and more
helpful to your friends, both living and dead, than anything
else you could do.
THE CLOUD OF UNKNOWING

How could a single desire for God be more helpful to my friends
than all the good works I might do for them? The dead ones I
can understand; the living want more from me. Was the author
of *The Cloud of Unknowing* just blowing off some spiritual hot air,
avoiding the hard and hazardous work of making the world a
better place? We have come full circle now, to once again be bit-
ten by the conflict between efficiency and love. My efficiency
mind says the only thing that counts is getting out there and
working for a better world. I need to stand up and be counted,
tackle injustice and sickness and poverty wherever it exists, stand
in the way of war, bend my back to the cause of freedom—and
do it quick and do it now and do it well.

The deep awakened heart within me offers no defense or justification of itself. It only desires and loves. It desires the same
things, and it hurts desperately with the passion and compassion
of its yearnings for a better world, but it cannot—or will not—
compete with efficiency. It only desires and loves.

My problem is pitting efficiency against love, struggling in the webs of either-or. It is always that way when efficiency gets the upper hand. When the how comes before the why, there can be nothing but tangles. One move for justice creates another injustice elsewhere; peace is bought in one place by fighting in another; revolution frees the oppressed, and they become oppressors; the hungry are fed and charged the price of their dignity; the ill are cured but not healed. When getting the job done is all that matters, the job that gets done creates more jobs that need doing.

Still the heart yearns, in simple, silent pleading, for action that does not mimic love but springs forth from it, for efficiency that is not an end in itself but a beginning of love's play, for love to reign over all service.

I think the author of the *Cloud* was right on target. My single desire for God will be of more help to my friends because my single desire for God will birth the kind of action that will really help them. It is not desiring God instead of doing helpful actions, but desiring God as the source of the actions that are going to be really helpful. It is that simple: put efficiency first, and the world gets to be the way it is today; put love first, and the whole meaning of efficiency is transformed.

Who knows what true, ultimate efficiency is? Who can discern the form of it, or where or when to do what? Look at the most loving acts that have been done for you—the ones you have no doubt about—and your own most loving acts for others. Where did they come from? Could they have been predicted? How would they have looked if they had come from somewhere outside a loving heart? Would they ever even have happened at all?

We used to live next door to a grouchy old man. He put up a chain link fence when our children began to play in the backyard. We tried to make friends with him, but he would have none of it. He threatened to kill my son Paul's kitten after it strayed into his rosebushes. "I see that cat on my land again, I'll poison it," he said. Paul, who was four at the time, became obsessed with keeping the kitten inside. He'd wake up screaming at night. A few days later the kitten was dead. We saw it die, and we were sure it had been poisoned. While the rest of the family was grieving and making up fantasies about what we could do for revenge, Paul grew very quiet. Finally he had something to say about our neighbor. "He must be very lonely. Maybe we should give him a birthday party or something."

Who could predict? Who can know what will bring peace and justice? When you hear or see a truly loving response, your heart says, "Ah, yes, that is right." That is what my family felt after the initial shock of Paul's words. But beforehand, *there is no way of telling what to do*. The problem is, we can't wait. We go running off half-cocked to take care of things, so caught up in the need to do that we ignore love altogether. We get ourselves into standoffs with our enemies and entanglements with our friends. We leap to rely on principles and policies instead of discernment. We react out of reflex and habit instead of responding from prayer, out of fear instead of love.

Even when our actions are patterned after the truly loving acts of others, they often bring as much trouble as healing. I could repeat my son's words every time someone hurt me, but they would not be quite right. Christians try to imitate Jesus' actions and follow the letter of his parables without attending to where Jesus' heart was turned at the time. It is ironic that so much of Christianity is just like the Pharisees Jesus challenged for following the letter of the Law with no thought of its source. We can be sure it is better to try to follow precepts and principles of loving-kindness than to give ourselves over to selfishness and revenge. But it is like stepping through the motions of a dance without ever hearing the music, copying the brush strokes of an artist without ever seeing the picture. It is the form of love without love's spirit. It is heartless.

Much of our heartlessness is reactive; we do it just because the world expects it. People at home and at work don't want to wait around for us to feel our hearts' desire. There is no time and no space. They want results now. And we think we should deliver. But it would not have to take long—just an interior glance would often be sufficient. My son was silent only for a few minutes before he hit us with his blockbuster.

Some of our heartlessness comes from addiction. Each of us has a repertoire of habitual ways of responding, for good or ill, to a wide variety of situations. We might try to justify such reflexive responses by saying they are more efficient than taking time to touch into a little open, loving presence. But don't believe it. We are just stuck in our ways, and that is addiction.

Most of our heartlessness, whether it is addictive, reactive, or just plain dumb, comes from fear. We are afraid of not meeting others' expectations. We are afraid of the agony, the uncertainty, and the terrifying space that come from refusing to act out an addiction. And, when we face right into it, we are afraid of what love is likely to call for. It might involve something beyond our control. It might mean getting hurt.

But the choice is ours. I am not being overzealous in saying that the only real hope for creation is for each of us human beings to attend to the yearnings of our hearts so that we can move forward in love instead of retreating or lashing out in fear. If we must sacrifice some of the world's efficiencies in order to find the time and space to do this, so be it. Further, we must attend our hearts with no ulterior motives: not so we will be finally more efficient, nor even so that we will have a better world. The attending must be an end in itself. As I have said, love cannot be a means to any end. Love is the lightning-spirit energy of the universe; it is something we join, not something we utilize. Somehow, there must be enough space between our desire for love and our automatic responses for us to participate in love's process. Otherwise we will overrun real love with our frantic attempts to be helpful.

Addictive Helpfulness

From a practical standpoint, we may need to consider a little abstinence from our automatic, reflexive responses of being helpful to others. For some of us, doing this may feel very threatening; to identify our addictions of helpfulness is to challenge the ways we habitually express love—it comes close to challenging our love itself. It is a tender business, but a most important one. I shall try to approach it as lightly as I can.

Let us say that someone we know is suffering. Perhaps this person is grieving, or having financial problems, or has just discovered his or her spouse is having an affair. We feel compassion and care for our friend; we want to do something to help. So far, so good; our hearts are compassionate, feeling the other person's pain and wanting to respond in a helping way. But immediately it is time to put the desire into action, and our addictions of helpfulness are triggered. In a very computerlike way, our internal programs of what-to-do-in-a-situation-like-this are accessed and run. In a very uncomputerlike way, we don't even take the time to see which program is called for. There is no time. We must be about the business of being helpful.

Understand me here; I dislike categorizing people into types. As with many old-time psychiatric labels, thinking of one another as types makes us less than human—more like machines with different functions. But it can be a lot of fun if you do it kindly, and that is the way I intend it now. I have made a list that categorizes some people by their habits of helpfulness.

There is the person who always wants to get you to talk about your troubles. I'll call this person the Empathophile; it is someone who seems convinced that everything can be made better by sharing. "Come over here, and tell me all about it."

I myself am a Technofixer. My immediate impulse is to get into your situation with my do-it-yourself repair kit. "Let me call your lawyer for you." "I know a place where you can get a low-interest loan." "Have you tried counting sheep?"

Then there's the Nuzzlecuddler. There is no problem so great that it can't be made better with a hug. Nuzzlecuddlers seldom say much; they just come at you with open arms and a silly smile. They are my favorites; I want at least one around whenever I am in trouble (or even when I'm not).

I also love Grub Fairies. No matter what the trouble is, they'll fix you something to eat. They are very straightforward, saying nothing about your problem, just, "I brought you a pie." There is a rare and wonderful subspecies called the Chocolate Grub Fairy. With a Chocolate Grub Fairy and a Nuzzlecuddler by my side, I think I could endure anything.

And of course there's the Portable Shoulder: they pull you to them and say, "Just let it all out."

The Theological Psychotic smiles reassuringly and then hits you with, "It's all God's will."

I could go on. I'd love to, but you get the point. Each of the styles—except for theological psychosis—can be helpful in its own way and at the right time, but who knows when or where? The problem is that they are automatic, undiscerned, reflexive. Most of us have a large enough community of support so that someone's style will really be helpful; the others just let us know people care. Besides, there is a God to see us through any deluge of misplaced helpfulness.

But let us go back for a moment and look at that tiny, perhaps almost nonexistent space between feeling a person's pain and doing something in response to it. It is not easy to just be with the pain of another, to feel it as your own. No wonder we are likely to jump into our habitual responses so quickly. As soon as we start doing something for or to the suffering person, we can minimize the bare agony of feeling that person's pain. It is like that everywhere; our addicted doings act as minor anesthesia.

There is, of course, a response and a style that avoids feeling another's pain altogether. It occurs all too often, and it is not at all funny. A dear and holy friend of mine died recently. He was a member of a religious community, but he died after years of suffering alone. He was old, sick, and a rascal, not easy to live with. The authorities of his order managed him, warehoused him and paid for his housing and medical care, but they could not be with him in his pain. They should have been his family, but they were not. He was alone. I feel angry with them, but I have a hefty plank in my own eye; I wonder how many state hospital patients I "managed" that way, how many patients on the surgical wards, how many prisoners?

"Well," you might say, "if your job is that of managing people—especially people in distress—you can't expect to feel everyone's pain. You'd burn out in no time if you let that happen." I tell you I do not think that is true. Feeling people's pain is *not* the cause of burnout. We burn out from our frenzied, addictive need to be doing something for or to them all the time. We burn out because we do not allow ourselves space between feeling and response. But burnout is hardly the point anyway. The point is love, in and for itself. And love needs space.

An Asceticism of Care

If we give ourselves more space between feeling and response, and enter that space in a consecrated way, we will find ourselves empowered for whatever response love calls for. I am sure of it.

The power then is not just ours; it is a nuclear fusion of divine grace and our dignified willingness.

Sometimes, perhaps often, taking the space will feel like an absence of response. We may fear the person will think we don't care because we are not immediately hopping like popcorn to do something helpful. And sometimes the response that is authentically invited will never appear overtly helpful. Perhaps we are just invited to pray, silently in the background, or just to be present without saying a word or offering even a touch. Sometimes love even invites us to leave a person alone. Such responses are not too good for our egos; the suffering person is unlikely to come and thank us for our lack of involvement. But love does not ask for credit, nor does it permit ego-gratification as the motive for response.

Authentic loving responsiveness calls for a kind of fasting from being helpful. Real helpfulness requires a relinquishment of our caretaking reflexes. It demands not only that we stay present with the unanesthetized pain of the person or situation, but that we also risk appearing to be uncaring. It further asks us to be unknowing. Right there in the center of a situation that screams for action, we must admit that we really don't know what to do. Finally, it invites us to turn our consciousness toward the exact point where our hearts are already looking: to the source of love. There, and only there, is the wellspring of authentic responsiveness found.

Discerning Response

I asked you to reflect upon discerning action in chapter 6, but there our emphasis was more on initiating action. Here we are looking at action in response to people and the world. The principles are the same, but the nuances may be different. Here expectations are placed upon us, and we have a host of ready-made habits to stave off. The discernment question now is, What really happens in the consecrated space between feeling and response?

From a small, self-centered viewpoint we could say a kind of discernment does go on. We stand there, with pain around us and uncertainty within us, and have only our hearts' desire to cling to. We look Godward in our unknowing and ask for guidance. What is love calling for? What would God have us do? How should we even pray? It doesn't happen in so many words, especially not in a crisis. But it is like a simple opening, filled only with wanting the right thing, stretching toward the source of love. It is not contrived, so there is no way to do it. It just happens, from our being there with things as they are and our refusal to escape into programmed response.

Authorities in discernment are fond of saying how it requires all our faculties: our thoughts, feelings, memories, everything. But I do not think *any* faculties are called for right here and now in this space. At least we could not call upon them intentionally; to do so would be to take ourselves somewhere beyond immediacy. Here there is nothing but the ache of love's desire: hoping for something, something graced, something good, something healing, something wonderful. Here a four-year-old is as good a theologian as you or I. Here a mentally retarded or emotionally handicapped person might even have an advantage, might be a window more open to the Spirit's breeze.

I cannot think of words; I can only imagine a reaching out of one's arms, opening, stretching, reaching to receive the touch of the holy. Christians pray with their hands held together; Muslims pray with their foreheads to the ground. But the old Hebrew posture shows it best for me: arms up, palms open, shoulders almost shrugged in dignified supplication. Here, in the space between feeling and response, there may well be no idea of prayer at all. The prayerfulness is inherent, given, in the very posture of one's heart.

Although I have tried to describe my image of the space, in fact I do not know what happens there. You do not know either, and will not if you enter the space with full consecration. Something happens, and it happens more unconsciously than consciously. Perhaps our hearts receive a word; perhaps we only listen to our hearts—who knows? God only knows. But something happens. It does not usually come through our intellect or feeling in such a way that we could say, "This is what I am meant to do." Instead, the thing is just there.

You need to explore this territory for yourself, but I can tell you how it is for me. Rarely, the thing presents itself as an idea, feeling, or intuition, something I could think about for a while. If so, and if there's time, *that's* when I bring my faculties to bear on it. Does it really feel right, even though it may not be what I or anyone else would have expected? Does it harmonize with past experiences of grace? Does it fit with my faith, and with my common sense? If not, is there some evidence that it's meant to be anyway? And on it can go, for as long as is needed, time permitting.

Far more often, the "something" comes in the space just as the next thing to do. It is sort of like a baby desire; a newborn yearning that has just a little quality of my heart's longing. It has a certain naturalness to it, even though it may be radically different from anything I could have predicted. But it bypasses commentary and is just there as an action ready to be taken. And, God willing, I just do it: I just yield into its birth with no reflection, nor even any hesitation if it's not too terribly bizarre. I act without thinking, yes indeed, but not without presence. In those moments when grace comes, the addictive patterns are put on hold, the space opens, and I just do the thing that is there to do. Or is it done through me in my willingness? The difference seems to have lost its significance.

If the thing does seem bizarre (like cracking a joke while someone is crying, or ignoring someone's heartfelt sharing), I hesitate. Sometimes it is so bizarre it scares me enough to retreat to some old tried-and-true addictive response. But if God grants my wits to be about me, I take that bizarre thing right back into the space from which it came and hold it in my opening, stretching Godward hands as if to say, "Really?" Again, if there's time, I may reflect a little. Is this a conditioned thing creeping in, masquerading as an inspiration? Does it have a certain aroma of familiarity? For example, I have a habit of using humor to deal with stress. Is that perhaps why I want to make this smart-aleck remark right now?

So I hold the little baby something for a while, turning it gently, offering it up. I try to trust that I can yield into its birth into action if and when the time is right, and that God's grace will carry everyone through even if I miss the moment. I am certain I miss a lot of moments this way. It is a certain fearful conservatism in me that goes back at least as far as the Hippocratic oath; first do no harm. To tell the truth, I don't think fearful conservatism ever helps one bit. It seems much more addictive than loving in the light of the holy space between feeling and response. But usually, after just a little holding back on my part, the baby is born. And then it is the next immediate moment.

What if nothing whatsoever comes in that space? God willing, I wait. I keep my big mouth shut and my meddling hands still and wait. Sometimes the waiting is beautiful in its spacious presence to what is, but more often it feels like a great struggle. It is a fierce and holy dignity to wait in the midst of things needing to be done and nothing but emptiness inside. It is even sometimes a kind of spiritual warfare, filled with temptations to do something, anything, to make a difference in the world outside and fill the void within. For me, whether the waiting is beautiful or agonizing, it is almost never boring.

When I meditate alone and think it is just for my own spiritual growth, the waiting can be boring. But in the midst of things, when people want responses and the world cries out for justice, there is no boredom. If for no other than selfish reasons, then, it makes sense to think of your personal practice as being for the sake of others. Creation needs your presence—now!

Expansive Presence

In chapter 6 I suggested you reflect on your own wisdom about the differences between impulses, compulsions, whims, and natural spontaneity. You might want to think about it again now, in the light of responding to the needs of the world around you. Recall specific times when you responded from automatic, conditioned habit. What did it feel like inside when you did that? Think of times when you have responded impulsively, on a whim. What did that feel like? And recall moments of naturally arising true spontaneity, born of the spaciousness between feeling and response. What was that like? Spend some time with your own real-life experiences. Turn them over in your hands. Think about them. Feel and taste and smell them. Get to know them well. In a flash, then, you may recognize one from another. It won't be with certainty, but it will be close enough. It will be sufficient, because you are not alone.

You can trust the process if your desire is solid. Let me put it another way: find your heart as best you can, follow it toward the source of love as much as possible, consecrate yourself, and trust. God's grace is present, God's love is irrevocable, and you can trust it and trust yourself within it.

There are no exceptions. There are no places inside you or in the whole of creation where God's love does not exist. It is alive in prisons and hospital wards, in concentration camps and foxholes, in earthquakes and hurricanes, in your own selfishness and addictions. It is always crying out to your heart, and your heart is awake, responding. Seek it and trust it.

Trust it, or risk it, as the case may be, in solitude, at home, at work, in play, in relationships, in pain, in grief, in laughter. Just as there are no exceptions in the places of creation, there are none in the moments and phases of your life. You never know what form love will take, but you can trust that it is there, and you can trust your desire for it.

Creation needs you for your love; love needs you for your creation. God needs you for yourself. Your heart has a sense of it already, and it is ready to join the flow of grace to guide you into ever-expanding presence. Seek the presence of love everywhere. Let there be no dark corners. Seek it inside and outside, in pride and shame, in tenseness and ease. Seek it in business meetings, shopping malls, the dentist's office, and courts of law. Look for it in school and at the municipal zoo, in your bathroom, in the factory, on the subway, at the beach, and in the mountains.

Know that there will be both joy and pain in the seeking and the finding. Things will change and become more free. Freedom sometimes hurts and is nearly always frightening. It involves a loss of that which bound you, and therefore you will grieve. Your relationships will change; as you claim more of the truth of your own heart, your attachment to other people will lighten. You may feel—and they may feel—that you are drifting away. But in a strange way you are really coming closer to them. You can trust it. The systems of your life will react against you, because you are less a slave of stability. You will not be able to defend yourself, but you will be protected. You can trust God's love.

You can trust God's love always and everywhere. There is much evil in the world, much confusion and bondage in yourself. Indeed, you are capable of being mean. But there is no meanness in your consecration; there is no vengeance in your true heart. Seek that heart, and the love in which it always is, and in which you can trust through all things.

It will hurt, and there may be times in the future that it will hurt more than it ever did in the past. There will be times of dark confusion and doubt. But you can still trust and risk—you *will* still trust and risk.

Julian of Norwich's most famous words are, "All shall be well, and all shall be well, and all manner of thing shall be well." This is no pie in the sky; it is solid truth from a fourteenth-century woman who is now considered one of the great theologians for our time. She heard the words in her visions of Jesus, on her sickbed at the age of thirty. Jesus told her, "You will not be overcome." She was very specific as she described her vision: "He did *not* say, 'You will never have a rough passage, you will never be over-strained, you will never feel uncomfortable,' but he *did* say, 'You will never be overcome.'"[1]

Julian pondered over her visions for nearly twenty years. Then, in a moment that must have sparkled with a smile, God asked her if she'd like to know what it all meant. She closed her book with what she learned, and with a certain presumption I will also close with it; the meaning, God willing, is the same.

Love was the meaning.

Who showed it to you? Love.

What was shown to you? Love.

Why was it shown to you? For Love.

Keep yourself in that love and you will learn more of it, And you will never learn anything else—ever![2]

Notes

Preface

Epigraph: *The Cloud of Unknowing and the Book of Privy Counseling*, trans. William Johnston (New York: Doubleday, 1973), p. 141.

1. See 1 Chronicles 28:9.

Chapter 1: Bearing the Beams of Love

Epigraph: William Blake, *Poems and Prophecies* (New York: Dutton, 1970), p. 10.

1. Paul MacLean, quoted in Richard M. Restak, *The Brain* (New York: Bantam, 1984), pp. 136–37.
2. François Fénelon, quoted in Brother Lawrence, *The Practice of the Presence of God*, trans. John J. Delaney (New York: Doubleday, 1977), p. 18.
3. The fourteenth-century mystic Jan van Ruysbroek, quoted by Evelyn Underhill in *An Anthology of the Love of God*, ed. Lumsden Barkway and Lucy Menzies (Wilton, CT: Morehouse-Barlow, 1976), p. 33.

Chapter 2: The Life of the Heart

Epigraph: Francis de Sales, *Treatise on the Love of God*, 11.20, trans. John Ryan (Rockford, IL: Tan, 1975), vol. 2, p. 253.

1. In Sanskrit, the ways are *yogas* (yokes or unions) or *margas* (ways or paths). *Karma marga* is the way of action or good works, corresponding to the Western way of the good. *Jnana marga* is the way of knowledge: the way of the true. *Bhakti marga*, the way of devotion, is most associated with feeling and corresponds to the Western way of the beautiful. The contemplative fourth way, *raja marga*, integrates the first three and includes the all-encompassing mystery beyond them. A more recent development, brought to fullness in Tibetan Buddhism, is known in Sanskrit as *mahamudra* (literally, "great seal" or "great posture"), or *rDzogs-chen* in Tibetan. For the seminal notion that the fourth way is contemplation, I am indebted to Joan

Hickey, Lindsley Ludy, and Cecilia Braveboy, who developed the idea as part of the Shalem Institute's project on spiritual formation in local churches.

2. Manjusrimitra, *Primordial Experience,* trans. Namkhai Norbu and Kennard Lipman (Boston: Shambala, 1986), p. xii. Thomas Kelly, *A Testament of Devotion* (New York: Harper & Row, 1941), p. 31. Contemplation will be described more fully later in the text, and I have given the term further treatment in *Addiction and Grace,* (San Francisco: Harper & Row, 1988), pp. 107–8, and in *Will and Spirit* (San Francisco: Harper & Row, 1982), pp. 24–26.

3. Abraham Isaac Kook, *The Lights of Penitence, The Moral Principles, Lights of Holiness, Essays, Letters, and Poems,* trans. Ben Zion Bokser (New York: Paulist, 1978), p. 207. Ibn al-'Arabi, *The Bezels of Wisdom,* trans. R. W. J. Austin (New York: Paulist, 1980), p. 148.

4. Much thought has been given to the differences between romantic and other kinds of love. Some exposition of this, including references to the work of Anders Nygren, Erich Fromm, and others, appears in chap. 6 of *Will and Spirit,* pp. 126–71.

5. *Attachment* literally means "nailed to." Addictions are the behavioral states produced by the process of attachment. See *Addiction and Grace,* esp. pp. 3–9.

6. Chogyam Trungpa, *Cutting Through Spiritual Materialism* (Berkeley, CA: Shambala, 1973), p. 49.

7. Romans 8:19.

8. Abraham Isaac Kook, *Orot Hakodesh* (Jerusalem: Agudah Lehotzoat Sifre Harayah Kook, 1938), vol. 2, p. 484.

9. Claude Bernard, quoted in Eric Kandel and James Schwartz, eds., *Principles of Neural Science* (New York: Elsevier Science Publishing, 1985), p. 612. Bernard created the famous term *internal milieu* to describe the body's inner environment, which can be regulated directly, as distinguished from our exterior environment, which must be influenced indirectly. Developing Bernard's ideas, Walter Cannon at Harvard stated that the hypothalamus functions upon the interior environment not so much to maintain constancy as "limited variability" (quoted in Kandel and Schwartz, eds. *Principles,* p. 612). This is an important distinction, as it acknowledges the essential flexibility of living organisms.

10. *Addiction and Grace,* pp. 77–83.

Chapter 3: Freedom and Intention

Epigraph: Carlos Castaneda's Yaqui sorcerer Don Juan, in *The Fire from Within* (New York: Simon & Schuster, 1984), p. 295. Italics are the author's; I have substituted "humanity" for the original "man."

1. Dag Hammarskjöld, *Markings* (New York: Alfred A. Knopf, 1966), p. 205.
2. Isaiah 43:1 and 4.
3. Kook, *Lights of Penitence*, p. 211.
4. Kook, *Lights of Penitence*, pp. 211–12.
5. The idea of *haqqodesh*, "holy ground," has many usages, but it consistently refers to Exodus 3:3–5. Moses sees the burning bush and says to himself, "I must go and look at this strange sight." He starts to move toward the bush when God speaks: "Come no nearer. Take off your shoes, for the place on which you stand is holy ground." It is very significant that God waits until Moses chooses to move toward the bush before speaking. The common interpretation is that the earth surrounding the bush is holy because it is where God is appearing. I wonder, is the ground of Moses' intention also holy because God is also appearing in Moses' choice to move forward?
6. Kandel and Schwartz, eds., *Principles of Neural Science*, pp. 218, 609–70.
7. Augustine of Hippo, *The Confessions of Saint Augustine*, trans. F. J. Sheed (New York: Sheed & Ward, 1943), pp. 235–36. John of the Cross, "The Living Flame of Love," verse 4, in *The Collected Works of Saint John of the Cross*, trans. Kieran Kavanaugh and Otilio Rodriguez (Washington, DC: ICS Publications, 1979), p. 718. Teresa's words are from paragraph 19 of her "Meditations on the Song of Songs," in Saint Teresa of Avila, *The Collected Works*, vol. 2, trans. Kieran Kavanaugh and Otilio Rodriguez (Washington, DC: ICS Publications, 1980), p. 230.
8. I am indebted to JoAnne Taylor for reminding me of this wonderful story in her equally wonderful study of the spiritual wisdom of children: *Innocent Wisdom: Children as Sriritual Guides* (New York: Pilgrim Press, 1989). I highly recommend this little book.
9. Song of Songs 5:2. Gregory of Nyssa, "Commentary on the Song of Songs," in Jean Daniélou, ed., *From Glory to Glory: Texts from Gregory of Nyssa's Mystical Writings*, trans. Herbert Musurillo (London: John Murray, 1963), p. 41.
10. Brother Lawrence, *The Practice of the Presence of God*, trans. Sr. Mary David (New York: Paulist, 1978), p. 89.

11. "We are to love, then, because God loved us first" (1 John 4:19).

Chapter 4: The Consecration of Hope

Epigraph: Julian of Norwich, *Revelations of Divine Love* (Sloane Manuscript, chap. 59), quoted in F. C. Happold, *Mysticism: A Study and an Anthology* (Baltimore, MD: Penguin, 1970), p. 325.

1. For more on willingness, see *Will and Spirit*, pp. 1–21. For consecration, see *Addiction and Grace*, pp. 149–52.

2. Genesis 28:16; Matthew 6:34 and Luke 21:36; Augustine, *Confessions*, quoted in Happold, *Mysticism*, pp. 231, 234; Brother Lawrence, *Practice of the Presence of God*, trans. Delaney, p. 48; Jean-Pierre de Caussade, *The Sacrament of the Present Moment*, trans. Kitty Muggeridge (San Francisco: Harper & Row, 1982), p. 81; Kelly, *Testament of Devotion*, p. 31; Thich Nhat Hanh, *The Miracle of Mindfulness*, trans. Mobi Warren (Boston: Beacon, 1976), and *Present Moment Wonderful Moment*, (Berkeley, CA: Parallax Press, 1990).

3. Caussade, *Sacrament of the Present Moment*, p. 62; Kelly, *Testament of Devotion*, p. 111; Thich Nhat Hanh, *Being Peace* (Berkeley, CA: Parallax, 1987).

4. I described this material in greater depth in "To Bear the Beams of Love: Contemplation and Spiritual Growth," *The Way*, Supplement, no. 59 (Summer 1987): pp. 24–34.

5. For more on the causes and dynamics of spiritual selfishness, or what I have called "spiritual narcisscism," see chap. 5 of my *Care of Mind/Care of Spirit* (San Francisco: Harper & Row, 1982), and chap. 5 of *Will and Spirit*.

6. The spiritual life that can begin in recovery at some point threatens the idolatry of recovery, and sometimes relapse may be necessary to move beyond the idolatry. I have discussed this at greater length in "Lightness of Soul: From Addiction Toward Love in John of the Cross," *Spiritual Life*, forthcoming, 1991.

7. Thomas Merton, *Love and Living*, ed. Naomi Burton Stone and Patrick Hart (New York: Bantam, 1980), p. 16.

8. For many Christians, the stewardship image drawn from Jesus' parables gives fodder to this servant-master sense of relationship with God. Look at the stories closely; Jesus is speaking about the *reign of heaven* being like what happens in the story as a whole. He is not equating God with the master.

You don't call that kind of master "Abba," and you don't call that kind of servant "friend" (John 15:15).

9. The word *discretion* comes from the same roots as *discernment*. We will explore discernment in chapters 6 and 12.

Chapter 5: Entering the Emptiness

Epigraph: Augustine of Hippo, *Confessions*, 1.1, quoted in *Augustine of Hippo: Selected Writings*, trans. Mary Clark (New York: Paulist, 1984), p. 9

1. The definition of the *YS* root and its derivatives comes from John L. McKenzie, *Dictionary of the Bible* (New York: Macmillan, 1965), p. 760. The Hebrew name *Yeshua* (Jesus), common in New Testament times, literally means "God is saving us." The homemaking reference is from John 15:4, "Make your home in me as I make mine in you."

2. I use the term *soul* in the original Hebrew sense of *nephesh*, the essence of a person. See *Will and Spirit*, p. 32.

3. Tilden Edwards, *Sabbath Time* (New York: Seabury, 1982).

4. Manjusrimitra, *Primordial Experience*, p. 32.

5. Erica Jong, *Any Woman's Blues* (New York: HarperCollins, 1990), pp. 133–34.

6. Etty Hillesum, *An Interrupted Life* (New York: Washington Square Press, 1985), pp. 27, 30.

7. Frederick Douglass, "Narrative of the Life of Frederick Douglass, an American Slave," excerpted in Abraham Chapman, ed., *Black Voices* (New York: New American Library, 1968), pp. 241–55.

8. Rainer Maria Rilke, *Letters to a Young Poet*, trans. M. D. Herder Norton (New York: W. W. Norton, 1954), pp. 35, 38.

9. From chaps. 79, 82, and 86 of the long version of her "Shewings" (from Sloane Manuscript 2499), in Julian of Norwich, *Revelations of Divine Love*, trans. Clifton Wolters (New York: Penguin, 1982), pp. 203, 208, 212.

Chapter 6: Practice

Epigraph: Psalm 57, excerpts from verses 7 and 8.

1. *The I Ching, or Book of Changes*, trans. Richard Wilhelm and Cary F. Baynes (New York: Bollingen Foundation, 1967), pp. xlix–lviii.

Chapter 7: The Little Interior Glance

Epigraph: Brother Lawrence, *Practice of the Presence of God*, trans. John J. Delaney, p. 87.

1. Brother Lawrence, *Practice of the Presence of God*, trans. John J. Delaney, pp. 46–47.
2. I have discussed this further in *Addiction and Grace*. See pp. 94 and 116.
3. Jeremiah 29:13–14. I am indebted to Joe Knowles for the hide-and-seek image.
4. Even if you believe in reincarnation, you only get to go around maybe six or seven thousand times—so you'd better take your foolishness seriously.
5. I could pepper you with remarks about "dysfunctional asceticism," but will only say it sounds like my kind of spirituality.
6. Matthew 6:34.
7. Habituation is the natural neurological process by which we come to ignore repetitive stimuli within and around us. See *Addiction and Grace*, pp. 75–77.

Chapter 8: The Prayer of the Heart

Epigraph: *Cloud of Unknowing*, p. 56.

1. Some of this historical sequence was obtained from John B. Noss, *Man's Religions* (New York: Macmillan, 1956).
2. "Directions to Hesychasts," in *Writings from the Philokalia on Prayer of the Heart*, trans. E. Kadloubovsky and G. E. H. Palmer (London: Faber & Faber, 1967), pp. 164–270.
3. *The Living Talmud*, trans. Judah Goldin (New York: New American Library, 1957), pp. 112–13.
4. Jaideva Singh, *Vijñanabhairava* (Delhi: Motilal Banarsidass, 1979), pp. 162–63. To be a little more precise, the breath silently says "ah" or "hahh" coming in, "m" or "mm" at the rest point between in-breath and out-breath, and "sah" going out. Taken together, the syllables form *hahmsah* or *hamsa*.
5. *Writings from the Philokalia*, p. 238.

Chapter 9: Loving the Source of Love

Epigraph: a repeated verse of the Song of Songs. This version is from the highly recommended new translation by Marcia Falk, *The Song of Songs*

(San Francisco: HarperCollins, 1990), stanzas 8, 13, 25.

1. Psalm 139:7, 9.
2. Jesus' words here are from John 15:15.
3. Matthew 18:3.
4. *Abba,* the Hebrew appellation connoting respectful, easy, loving familiarity.
5. Martin Buber, *I and Thou,* trans. Walter Kaufman (New York: Charles Scribners' Sons, 1970), pp. 130–31.
6. Erich Fromm, I think, was first to publish that most helpful distinction between "I love you because I need you" and "I need you because I love you." *The Art of Loving* (New York: Harper & Bros., 1956).
7. McKenzie, *Dictionary of the Bible,* p. 834.
8. Evelyn Underhill, "Love and Response," in *Anthology of the Love of God,* p. 30.
9. John of the Cross, "The Spiritual Canticle," in *Collected Works,* pp. 713–15. In these holy verses, God is every bit as caught by love as John is: "It captivated You," John says to God, "and one of my eyes wounded You."
10. The story about Origen is probably apocryphal, but men have castrated themselves and women have physically wounded themselves in attempting to cope with spiritual passion.
11. Song of Songs 8:1.
12. Elizabeth of the Trinity, *The Complete Works,* vol. 1, trans. Aletheia Kane (Washington, DC: ICS Publications, 1984), pp. 179 and 181 n. The full phrase was even more radical:"Let yourself be loved more than these." Elizabeth wrote the word *let* in larger letters to communicate her increasing emphasis.
13. Buber, *I and Thou,* pp. 14–15.
14. Acts 17:28, Ephesians 1:23, Exodus 3:14.
15. Luke 21:36.
16. John of the Cross, *Collected Works,* pp. 66–67.

Chapter 10: Contemplative Presence

Epigraph: Buber, *I and Thou,* p. 143.
1. John 13:25; 21:20.
2. It does make for a little more orthodox Christian practice to cover the Holy Trinity as my examples suggest: body in the arms of its Creator, breath being breathed by the Spirit, mind given to the Christ, and all then becoming one loving presence.

3. Luke 10:38–42.

Chapter 11: Loving in the World

Epigraph: Hildegard of Bingen, *Meditations with Hildegard of Bingen*, trans. Gabriele Uhlein (Santa Fe, NM: Bear and Company, 1982), p. 70.
1. Hildegard of Bingen, *Meditations*, p. 99.
2. Psalms 17:8; 36:7; 57:1; 63:7. See also Matthew 23:37 and Luke 13:34.
3. Hanh, *Miracle of Mindfulness*, p. 24.

Chapter 12: Loving for the World

Epigraph: *Cloud of Unknowing*, p. 60.
1. Julian of Norwich, "All shall be well" quoted in Happold, *Mysticism*, p. 329. "You will not be overcome" quoted in *Revelations of Divine Love*, trans. Wolters, p. 185. For a discussion of her theological impact today, see *A Lesson of Love: The Revelations of Julian of Norwich*, trans. John-Julian (New York: Walker, 1988), pp. v–xvii.
2. This is my version of lines from Julian's last (86th) chapter. Each of the three sources mentioned above offers a different translation of her Chaucerian English.

Index of Exercises and Reflection Questions

General Index